D0327173

T. S. ELIOT
The Dialectical Structure
of His Theory of Poetry

FEI-PAI LU

T. S. ELIOT
The Dialectical Structure
of His Theory of Poetry

The University of Chicago Press / Chicago & London

Acknowledgment is made to Harcourt, Brace & World, Inc., for permission to quote from *Selected Essays, Four Quartets, From Poe to Valéry,* and *Essays on Elizabethan Drama* by T. S. Eliot; to Faber and Faber, Ltd., for *Collected Poems 1909–62, The Use of Poetry and the Use of Criticism, After Strange Gods, Elizabethan Essays, The Idea of a Christian Society, Notes towards the Definition of Culture,* and *For Lancelot Andrewes;* and to Methuen & Co., Ltd., and Barnes & Noble, Inc., for *The Sacred Wood.* Selections from *On Poetry and Poets* are reprinted by permission of Farrar, Straus & Giroux, Inc. Copyright © 1945, 1951, 1956, 1957 by T. S. Eliot.

Standard Book Number: 226-49628-7

Library of Congress Catalog Card Number: 66-13877

The University of Chicago Press, Chicago 60637

The University of Chicago Press, Ltd., London

In Memory of
My Beloved
Father and Mother

More often, though, we miss a point or confuse an argument by failing to see that under the attractively novel phrasing, and behind its special graces, we have to do with the same familiar joints and muscles and bones.

I. A. RICHARDS, *How to Read a Page*

Although there is but one Center, most men live in centers of their own.

HERACLITUS, *Cosmic Fragments*

Preface

This book is intended to be a systematic analysis of T. S. Eliot's criticism. It tries to show what kind of critical problems Eliot had raised and the method involved in his solution of such problems. My intellectual obligations to the "Chicago School" of critics are beyond acknowledgment. I am especially grateful to Professors R. S. Crane, Elder Olson, and George Williamson, who have read through this book in its original form as a dissertation. Professor Olson even took the trouble to suggest many stylistic improvements for my completed manuscript. To Professor Richard McKeon I owe an hour of delightful discussion on Eliot. Thanks are due to Professor Gwin J. Kolb, who together with Professor Olson and Professor Williamson, recommended the publication of this book. I also want to thank Professor W. A. Jackson of Harvard University for extending me the freedom of using the Eliot Collection at Houghton Library. The courtesies of the Houghton Library staff made my sojourns at Harvard the most pleasant episodes in the earlier stages of this study. But my deepest gratitude goes to my wife Lydia and my sister Shung-chao; without their heroism this book could never have been written.

Contents

1

Introduction:
The Commentators' Vistas

SKEPTICS AND ECLECTICS

Even a decade ago, T. S. Eliot was already regarded as one of those "over-written" authors. The sentiment that everything that needed to be said had been said reverberated throughout the lines of David Daiches' modest protestation when he wrote, in 1949, for the *Yale Review:*

> On the bookshelves of the modern student of literature stand[s] T. S. Eliot's "Collected Poems, 1909–1935," followed by his later publications, the whole flanked by volumes of critical studies from F. O. Matthiessen to the anthologies of Leonard Unger and B. Rajan. If he wishes to know the true meaning of the "Waste Land," he can look it up in Cleanth Brooks's essay; James Johnson Sweeney and Helen Gardiner between them will tell him how to read the "Four Quartets"; Miss Bradbrook and Mr. Ransom will put the pro's and con's of Eliot as a critic, while Mario Praz will tell the source of his Dante criticism. There are also individual guides to his imagery, his ideas, his influence, his significance for the history of poetry and of literary taste, his importance as (in Delmore Schwartz's excited phrase) a "culture hero." The student can, if he wishes, go further back and attack the earlier academic

1

detractors of Eliot with F. R. Leavis or see his greatness asserted with devoted enthusiasm by Matthiessen. What is left to be said?[1]

The corpus of commentaries on Eliot was far more bulky than Daiches was aware of, and is still bulkier than he dared to expect.[2] In addition to the long list of articles and books, we can now count at least half a score of doctoral dissertations which are wholly or substantially devoted to the study of Eliot's criticism alone.[3] It is only natural that before embarking upon another account, one should be alert to the labors of his predecessors, the benefits he might derive from them, and the lessons he might draw.

Nearly all of Eliot's commentators professed interest in his critical "method"; but evidently not all those who made such profession were interested in Eliot's critical judgments, or in the doctrines that give support to such judgments, or in the grounds on which the doctrines themselves are justified, or in the procedure and operation of such justification. Bertram Higgins, for instance, addressed himself to "The Critical Method of T. S. Eliot"; however, it was Eliot's rhetorical efficacy that actually received his attention.[4] What interested Higgins was not criticism but the verbal presentation of it. Similarly, M. C. Bradbrook's essay, "Eliot's Critical Method," was primarily a study of Eliot's stylistic devices.[5] Taking a cue from the rhetorician's classification into the high, low, and middle styles, Miss Bradbrook immediately identified Eliot's "method" as "neutral." A

[1] David Daiches, "T. S. Eliot," *Yale Review*, XXXVIII (1949), 460.

[2] See Bibliography, "Commentaries on Eliot's Criticism."

[3] See Bibliography, "Dissertations on Eliot's Criticism."

[4] B. Higgins, "The Critical Method of T. S. Eliot," *Scrutinies*, ed. Edgell Rickwood, II (London, 1931), 54–71.

[5] M. C. Bradbrook, "Eliot's Critical Method," *Focus Three: T. S. Eliot*, ed. B. Rajan (London, 1947), pp. 119–28.

neutral method, according to her, neither coerces through the rigor of reason nor persuades by emotional appeals. It simply elucidates.

The rhetoricians were well in agreement about the characteristic powers of Eliot's prose. But concerning Eliot's critical judgments, disagreements were frequent and even violent. Eliot's early indictment of Milton's "magniloquence" as a pernicious poetic influence, for instance, aroused Logan Pearsall Smith's wrath.[6] For Smith, however, critical judgment is purely a matter of scholarship and taste. He is not in the least interested in the theory which conditions Eliot's judgments and gives meaning to his statements.

Indeed, whether Eliot's criticism forms a coherent whole —whether it is controlled by a consistent body of doctrines and principles and formulated in pursuance of a uniform procedure—remains, for most of his commentators, an open question. Reviewing *The Sacred Wood* in 1921, Conrad Aiken found himself compelled to call Eliot's critical formulations "unscientific," since Eliot by turns affirmed and denied "personality" as a determinant of artistic form.[7] Complaints about Eliot's contradiction and confusion, incoherence and inconsistency grew in force with the lapse of years. Honest bewilderment was expressed and useful doubts were raised by L. C. Knights, Humphrey House, F. L. Lucas, Arthur Quiller-Couch, J. C. Ransom, F. W. Bateson, and Lewis Freed; and the lists of "conflicting statements" and "mysterious distinctions" in Eliot supplied by Eastman, Winters, Robbins, Mordell, and Austin were massive.[8]

---

[6] Logan Pearsall Smith, *Milton and His Modern Critics* (Boston, 1941).

[7] Conrad Aiken, "The Scientific Critic," *The Freeman*, II (1921), 593–94.

[8] L. C. Knights, "Shakespeare and Shakespeareans," *Scrutiny*, III (1934), 306–14; Humphrey House, "Mr. Eliot as a Critic," *The New Oxford*

Solutions of Eliot's "confusions" (so far as attempted by his commentators) easily fell into two classical patterns, eclecticism and skepticism. The more tactful of the skeptics tried to minimize the importance of critical consistency through what Eliot himself would have called a "conspiracy of approval" by laying the entire value of his criticism on the intermittent appearances of his rare "insight" and unusual "intuition." The more strenuous of the skeptics cited Eliot's distaste for systems to prove how trivial systematic thinking was to him. And the more systematic of the skeptics questioned the utility and wisdom of systematic thinking as a whole. Whereas the skeptics dealt with the problem of Eliot's supposed critical confusions by denying the usefulness of critical theory, by asserting Eliot's unwillingness to pursue systematic thinking, and by trusting Eliot's intuition rather than his method, the eclectics selected whatever portion of his criticism appeared to them "coherent," "central," and "effective" for the express purposes of interpretation, refutation, or approval. Thus, well aware of Eliot's religious interests, Edmund Wilson, in 1931, still insisted:

> It becomes plainer and plainer, as time goes on, that the real effect of Eliot's, as of Valéry's, literary criticism, is to impose upon us a conception of poetry as some sort of pure

---

Outlook, I (1933), 95–105; F. L. Lucas, "Criticism," *Life and Letters*, III (1929), 433–65; Arthur Quiller-Couch, "Tradition and Orthodoxy," *The Poet as Citizen and Other Papers* (New York, 1935), pp. 44–66; J. C. Ransom, "T. S. Eliot: The Historic Critic," *New Criticism* (Norfolk, 1941), pp. 135–208; F. W. Bateson, "Dissociation of Sensibility," *Essays in Criticism*, I (1951), 302–12; Lewis Freed, *T. S. Eliot: Aesthetics and History*, (La Salle, Ill., 1962); Max Eastman, "The Swan Song of Human Letters," *Scribner's*, LXXXVIII (1930), 598–607; Yvor Winters, "T. S. Eliot, or the Illusion of Reaction," *The Anatomy of Nonsense* (Norfolk, 1943), pp. 120–67; R. H. Robbins, *The T. S. Eliot Myth* (New York, n.d.); Albert Mordell, *T. S. Eliot's Deficiencies as a Social Critic* (Girard, 1951); Allan Austin, "T. S. Eliot as Literary Critic" (Ph.D. dissertation, New York University, 1956).

and rare aesthetic essence with no relation to any of the practical human uses.[9]

And after all the debating over Eliot's "change," "development," "conversion," "recantation," and "apotheosis," Cleanth Brooks in *Literary Criticism: A Short History* still held that the essence of Eliot's poetic theory lay in his conception of poetry as organic metaphor and was epitomized in his doctrine of the objective correlative.[10] Thus after Eliot had been unanimously labeled as an unsystematic thinker, Kristian Smidt still admitted that there was little or no change in Eliot's "aesthetic ideas" and Mervyn K. Williamson still held that the autonomy of art remained the core of all Eliot's criticism.[11]

Eclecticism involves exclusion and translation, for the selection itself of what appears to be central and coherent entails some principle of selection. Such a principle provides grounds for the rejection of whatever, in terms of that principle, appears to be extraneous and irrelevant and supplies unity to whatever, again in terms of that principle, is intelligible and meaningful. Sister Mary Cleophas Costello, for instance, based her account of Eliot's poetic theory upon one single preoccupation: that is, namely, poetry as a verbal endeavor. For her, formulation of the nature of poetry must be a formulation of the nature of the language it employs. Sister Mary Cleophas made a dialectical distinction

---

[9] Edmund Wilson, "T. S. Eliot," *T. S. Eliot: A Selected Critique*, ed. L. Unger (New York, 1948), p. 189.

[10] Wiliam K. Wimsatt Jr. and Cleanth Brooks, *Literary Criticism: A Short History* (New York, 1957), esp. pp. 667, 676.

[11] Kristian Smidt, *Poetry and Belief in the Work of T. S. Eliot* (Oslo, 1949), p. 60; Mervyn Williamson, "A Survey of T. S. Eliot's Criticism: 1917–1956" (Ph.D. dissertation, University of Texas, 1958); cf. also Sister Mary Cleophas Costello, *Between Fixity and Flux* (Washington, D.C., 1947), p. 107.

of linguistic kinds: words are either cognitive or emotive; they are used either as discrete units or as members of organic discourse. Her definition of poetry results from a series of distinctions between verse and prose, prose and poetry, poetry and verse. According to Sister Mary Cleophas, "intensity" of sound structure separates verse from prose, affectivity differentiates poetry from prose, and "intensity" of meaning structure distinguishes poetry from verse and prose. The definition she arrived at and attributed to Eliot was a verbal definition: poetry consists in the intensity of structure in an emotive discourse. In the light of this definition she gathered evidences from Eliot's writings, reinterpreted Eliot's critical concepts, and resolved the "conflicting" critical traditions operative in Eliot—namely, the "Aristotelian" concern with "structure," the "Horatian" concern with "statement," and the "Romantic" concern with "affectivity."

> Eliot has modified the Horatian tradition of presenting a statement by emphasizing that what is important for poetry is not the statement as such but the accompanying affectivity of that statement. This would link his theory to a romantic theory of expression. Eliot has tried to avoid this by placing his *differentia* in the object at such moments as the ensemble of structural elements achieves such artistry that the affective meaning is clearly embodied in the work and an effect which he calls intensity is achieved. By stressing the making of this affectivity into a structure which uses words that refer to "objects, situations, or chains of events," he has introduced an element of the Aristotelian theory of art as the making of an object.[12]

The principle that guides Sister Mary Cleophas' translation was well enunciated. Less well articulated were the

---

[12] Costello, *op. cit.*, p. 106.

principles of translation operative in those writers who had
been directly or indirectly involved in the great debate over
Eliot's "conversion." Impressed by Eliot's analyses of poetry and the poet, and lured by such credos and dicta as the
autonomy of art and the use of the "objective correlative"
as a means of expression, early commentators, like John Middleton Murry (1921), Conrad Aiken (1921), Leonard
Woolf (1921), Marianne Moore (1921), Francis Fergusson
(1927), W. E. Collins (1931), and G. W. Stonier (1932),
were all convinced of the "aesthetic" orientation of Eliot's
"impersonal theory of poetry."[13] When Murry in 1921
summarized Eliot's criticism as "a criticism which is directed
towards a complete exploration of the work of literature
with a view to mastering its mechanism,"[14] he not only
spoke for the immediate responses of the reviewers to *The
Sacred Wood*, but also anticipated the popular notion (still
prevailing today) that Eliot started his career as a "pure"
aesthetic critic.

Commentators who had been insisting upon the "aesthetic" character of Eliot's poetic theory felt themselves
seriously challenged by two of his publications: *For Lancelot Andrewes: Essays On Style and Order* in 1927 and *After
Strange Gods: A Primer of Modern Heresy* in 1934. But
even as late as 1949, Kristian Smidt still held that "in spite
of the development that we have noticed, we find little or

---

[13] L[eonard] W[oolf], "Back to Aristotle," *Athenaeum*, No. 4729 (December, 1920), p. 834; Marianne Moore, "The Sacred Wood," *Dial*, LXX
(1921), 336–39; Aiken, *op. cit.*; John Middleton Murry, "The Sacred
Wood," *The New Republic*, XXVI (1921), 194–95; Francis Fergusson,
"T. S. Eliot and His Impersonal Theory of Art," *The American Caravan*,
ed. Van Wyck Brooks (New York, 1927), pp. 446–53; W. E. Collins,
"T. S. Eliot the Critic," *Sewanee Review*, XXXIX (1931), 419–24; G. W.
Stonier, "Eliot and the Plain Reader," *Fortnightly Review*, CXXXIII
(1932), 620–29.

[14] Murry, *op. cit.*, p. 195.

no change in Eliot's aesthetic ideas from first to last. His defense of the autonomy of poetry is maintained throughout."[15] Most commentators, however, subscribed to some theory of "conversion" from the "aesthetic" position to the "moralistic." J. C. Ransom, Yvor Winters, and Edward Greene, together with many others, proposed 1928 as the year of Eliot's conversion.[16] Bradbrook suggested 1929, which saw the publication of Eliot's *Dante*.[17] Delmore Schwartz, D. S. Savage, C. I. Glicksberg, and Kathleen Nott contended that Eliot's ethical criteria did not become operative in his literary criticism until the appearance of *After Strange Gods* in 1934.[18] Victor Brombert adduced evidences that led him to regard Eliot's change not as a sudden mutation but as a prolonged conflict between an impersonal aestheticism and a personal moralism. Summarizing his arguments, Brombert wrote:

> The fear of any aesthetic-ethical standard in criticism led Eliot to assert that from the point of view of ART only the aesthetic values were to be taken into consideration. Very soon, however, he had to concede that pure literature was only a chimera and that much entered into a work of art which could not be accounted for in purely aesthetic terms. Next, although insisting that the poet was not really a thinker, Eliot agreed that intellectual beliefs

[15] Smidt, *op. cit.*, p. 60.

[16] Ransom, *op. cit.*, p. 51; Winters, *op. cit.*, p. 102–3; Edward Greene, *T. S. Eliot et la France* (Paris, 1951), pp. 145, 171.

[17] M. C. Bradbrook, *T. S. Eliot* (London, 1950), p. 51: "During the later nineteen-twenties, Eliot published a number of essays, but the little monograph on Dante (1929) marks the next phase in his critical development."

[18] Delmore Schwartz, "The Literary Dictatorship of T. S. Eliot," *Partisan Review*, XVI (1949), 119–20; D. S. Savage, "The Orthodoxy of T. S. Eliot," *The Personal Principle* (London, 1944), p. 103; C. I. Glicksberg, "T. S. Eliot as Critic," *Arizona Quarterly*, IX (1948), 225; Kathleen Nott, *The Emperor's Clothes* (London, 1953), p. 7.

expressed in a poem could not be neglected. In his essay on Dante, Eliot maintained that the reader in order to appreciate the poetry, was not called upon to share but merely to understand the beliefs expressed. Then followed a series of concessions: first, that it was not possible in practice to separate appreciation from belief; secondly, that there existed poets who were simultaneously thinkers; thirdly, that the beliefs expressed stood in a definite relation to the greatness of the poetry; and finally, that the reader in order fully to judge and appreciate the poetry, could not leave out of account the beliefs and personality of the author himself.[19]

However different their opinions regarding the date and manner of Eliot's critical "conversion," these writers shared one common assumption: the dichotomy of art and morals. In simple terms, their procedure was as follows. They first divided Eliot's critical propositions and arguments into two equal portions, putting into one group (which they called "aesthetic") whatever appeared conformable to some preconceived notion of "art," and into another group (which they called "ethical") whatever harmonized with some preconceived notion of "morals." This done, they began to trace Eliot's critical development either as a matter of sudden mutation involving the replacement of the aesthetic principle by the moral principle, or as a course of prolonged conflict involving the alternative predominance of art and morals. This evidently is a variation of what I have called the eclectic method. Like all eclectic methods, it has recourse to the precarious practices of translation and exclusion—practices which at their best yield partial treatment and at their worst, downright perversion and reckless tagging. Eliot has been called by turns aesthete and moralist,

---

[19] Victor Brombert, *The Criticism of T. S. Eliot: Problem of an "Impersonal Theory of Poetry"* (New Haven, 1949), p. 33.

radical and reactionary, romanticist and classicist; his criticism has been alternatively accused of emotionalism and anti-emotionalism, intellectualism and anti-intellectualism. Some commentators—Brombert, Rooney, and Smidt—held that Eliot's poetic theory can be most profitably discussed in terms of his concept of "poetic belief" (content); some others—Vivas, Brooks, and Panicker—found Eliot's doctrine of "objective correlative" (form) the core of his theory of poetry. Even when the doctrine of objective correlative is agreed upon as the essence of Eliot's poetics, opinions are widely divided about its exact implication. For Cleanth Brooks, objective correlative means "organic metaphor"; for Sister Mary Cleophas Costello, "the intensity of meaning-structure." Eliseo Vivas takes it as a vehicle of expression for the poet's emotions; Allan Austin treats it as the poetic content to be conveyed by verbal expressions.[20] Such diversity of opinion does not necessarily reflect "confusion" on the part of Eliot. Instead, it testifies most eloquently to the varied interests and concerns of his commentators and the variety of principles which they had introduced for the purposes of interpretation, refutation, or approval.

Indeed, accounts of Eliot's critical development which take the dichotomy of art and morals as their basis of exposition are themselves but a compromise solution to what has been construed as Eliot's "confusions." The chief sources of irritation to the exegetes are not hard to locate. Complaints about Eliot's "confusions" easily fall under three heads: the equivocal character of his terms, his regular (or rather irregular) practice of denying and affirming the same

---

[20] Eliseo Vivas, "The Objective Correlative of T. S. Eliot," *The American Bookman*, I (1944), 7–18; Allan Austin, "T. S. Eliot's Objective Correlative," *The University of Kansas Review*, XXVI (1959), 133–40. Vivas' essay was reprinted in Robert W. Stallman (ed.), *Critiques and Essays in Criticism: 1920–1948* (New York, 1949), pp. 389–400.

proposition, and the apparent contradiction between his arguments. Whereas the eclectics sought to reconstruct, by a process of exclusion and translation, new coherent wholes out of this alleged critical chaos, the historians attempted to account for the inconsistencies in terms of change and development. Notwithstanding all the sincerity and diligence manifested, seldom did they realize that Eliot's "inconsistencies" had issued from philosophical roots and could never be satisfactorily explained on historical grounds. Only when Eliot's characteristic method is ascertained, only when the premises and procedure that condition the meaning of his terms and the validity of his arguments are illuminated, may the nature of his critical inconsistencies be fully understood.

DIALECTIC AS PRINCIPLE

Terms in Eliot's critical works are, indeed, equivocal and purposefully kept vague. "We should not try to pin a word down to one meaning, which it should have at all times, in all places, and for everybody," says Eliot in the "Aims of Education," when he tries to propose a definition for the word "education." "There are many words which we much use in slightly different senses in different contexts," he continues, "and the difference in meaning, though slight, may be very important."[21] Feeling, as Mr. Panicker clearly recognized, is a basic term in Eliot's critical system.[22] Eliot dichotomizes feeling into two kinds: the precise and the vague. As precise feelings are articulate and definite, so vague feelings are "tangled" and "chaotic." The precise feelings

---

[21] Eliot, "The Aims of Education, I: Can 'Education' Be Defined?" *Measure*, II (1950), 7.

[22] Rev. Geevarghese T. Panicker, "A Whole of Feeling: A Study of the Place of Emotion and Feeling in the Poetic Theory of T. S. Eliot" (abstract of Ph.D. dissertation, Catholic University of America, 1959), pp. 1–2.

are those that occupy definite places in a "pattern" of feelings; in other words, feelings that have acquired ideality in and through the process of unification. For in unification, feelings are "combined," relationships are developed; what used to be a tangible *that* becomes, in and through combination, an intelligible *what*. The precise feelings, therefore, are feelings that have been "transmuted." They are as intelligible and significant as they are concrete and tangible.

Feeling, in the more restricted sense of the word, denotes vague sensation; in its more comprehensive sense, it implies coincidence of intelligibility and tangibility. In his doctoral dissertation as well as in his critical writings, Eliot consistently argues that there is no sensation which is not a perception and that "not only knowledge, but all feeling, is in perception."[23] The distinction between sensation and thought is, in fact, merely a consequence of analysis. Because of this plurality of meanings, it is possible for Eliot to oppose feeling to sensation, emotion, and thought, and yet to combine it with them. Sometimes he allies feeling with impression, sensation, and emotion in opposition to thought (as actuality would oppose ideality); sometimes he combines emotion with thought in opposition to feeling (as ideality would oppose reality); and sometimes he merges feeling, emotion, and thought into one all-inclusive term such as experience or sensibility (which is at once ideal and real). In Eliot's dialectical scheme, poetry is freely treated

---

[23] Eliot, *The Sacred Wood* (2d ed.; London, 1928), p. 10; hereafter referred to as *SW*. "Prose and Verse," Chapbook, XXII (1921), 9: "The work of poetry is often said to be performed by the use of images. . . . This appears to be true, but it does not follow that there are two distinctive faculties, one of imagination and one of reason, one of poetry, and one of prose, or that 'feeling,' in a work of art, is any less an intellectual product than is 'thought.' "

as the permutation of feelings, the objectification of emotions, and the realization of thoughts.[24]

That "unity of experience" constitutes the matrix of
Eliot's critical dialectic has not escaped Professor R. S.
Crane.[25] The operation of Eliot's dialectical principle of
Unity has especially attracted those who were directly or
indirectly acquainted with Eliot's doctoral dissertation, "Experience and the Objects of Knowledge in the Philosophy
of F. H. Bradley."[26] Of those who took serious interest in
Eliot's dissertation, R. W. Church perhaps was the best
equipped.[27] Church enjoyed a firsthand knowledge of the

---

[24] In Eliot, emotion is by turns allied to and distinguished from thought
and feeling as it is variously analogized to the two states of perception
either as concrete sensation or as heightened consciousness. Artistic emotion is supposed to be "the emotional equivalent of thought," concrete
yet meaningful. And the intelligibility of artistic emotion renders it "precise," "definite," and "particular." The dialectical synthesis of ideality
and reality has been only slightly modified when Eliot treats poetry not
as a union of thought and emotion but as a union of significant emotion
and concrete imagery. Thus in "Hamlet and His Problems," (*SW*, pp. 95–
103), Eliot considers art work as an "objective correlative" of "precise"
emotion; asserts that only the "definite" and "particular" emotion can
give unity to the objective correlative; attributes the formlessness of
Hamlet to the indefiniteness of the emotion it tries to render; and traces
the confusion of the play back to the disorder of the poet's soul. For
greater elaboration of this series of contrasts in Eliot, see chap. ii, section one: "Transmutation."

[25] R. S. Crane, "Two Essays in Practical Criticism: A Prefatory Note,"
Kansas University Review, VIII (1942), 199–219.

[26] The dissertation is now available in print under the title *Knowledge
and Experience in the Philosophy of F. H. Bradley* (London, 1964).

[27] R. W. Church, "Eliot on Bradley's Metaphysics," *The Harvard Advocate*, CXXV (1938), 24–26; Hugh Kenner, *The Invisible Poet* (New
York, 1959), esp. pp. 40–69, 117–18; Eric Thompson, "Dissociation of Sensibility," *Essays in Criticism*, II (1952), 207–13; and *T. S. Eliot: A Metaphysical Perspective* (Carbondale, 1963) all deal with Bradley's influence
on Eliot's critical theory. Thompson's early article ably linked Eliot's
poetic theory to his doctoral dissertation and traced his doctrine of "unified sensibility" back to the epistemology of Bradley. "In the frame of
reference [Hegel-Bradley]," writes Thompson, "wherein Eliot is known
to have worked there is no such thing as mere sensation; every psychic
event whether a sensation, a feeling, an emotion, or an idea has two sides:

dissertation and he was a close student of Bradley. Moreover, like Eliot himself, Church was a pupil of Harold H.
Joachim, the Oxford philosopher who helped edit Bradley's
posthumous works.[28] In "T. S. Eliot on the Metaphysics of
Bradley," his summary of Eliot's dissertation, Church not
only suggests (after F. O. Matthiessen) the direct bearing
of the Bradleyan dialectic of relation and quality on Eliot's
concept of poetry as "unified sensibility," but also recognizes "experience" as the ground term of Eliot's philosophi-

---

a side that is felt and another that is thought. In that frame of reference,
moreover, 'mind' is not a 'faculty' for registering atom-like bits of experience. There is a universe which is Mind; the frame of that universe is reason, the matter is sentience. What human beings misleadingly call their
'minds' are finite centers diversely focusing, somewhat like Shelley's dome
of multi-colored glass, the white radiance of the Absolute. Thought is the
focussing and feeling is the focussed." Thompson's recent book, once
again, pressed the point that Eliot had derived his conception of poetry
from the epistemology of the dissertation. But, curiously enough, when
Thompson came to actual analysis of Eliot's poetics, he suddenly equated
it to R. G. Collingwood's theory of language as imaginative-expression.
"I must step outside Eliot's criticism," announced Thompson (p. 58),
"and resort to a formula taken from R. G. Collingwood's *Principle of Art.*
Collingwood's concept of art-as-language [which Eliot evidently read with
interest in the 1940's] seems very close to what Eliot might have come up
with had he been forced to propound a theory of art on an examination
in 1916." Thompson, however, must be commended for two things. First,
he noted in passing the "philosophical nuances of words like object, feeling, ideas, point of view as Eliot uses them" (p. 52). Moreover, he even
stated explicitly: "No term in Eliot's dissertation (with the possible ex-
ception of 'object') is more important than 'point of view'" (p. 23). Frye's
T. S. Eliot (London, 1963), pp. 43–44, contains a short but interesting account of Bradley's influence on Eliot.

[28] F. H. Bradley, *Ethical Studies* (2d ed.; Oxford, 1927), p. vii: "In
publishing this edition of *Ethical Studies* the sister and brother of the
author desire to offer their warm thanks to Prof. H. H. Joachim for his
valuable advice on many points, and especially for his help in the editing
of the new notes." Church mentioned in his *Bradley's Dialectic* (London,
1942), p. 10, that he had attended Joachim's seminars on Hegel and
Bradley. As for the relation between Eliot and Joachim, see T. S. Eliot,
"Prof. H. H. Joachim," *Times*, London (August 4, 1938), p. 12. Kenner
indicated (*op. cit.*, pp. 71, 76) that Eliot read the *Posterior Analytics* with
Joachim in 1915 when he was a holder of the Frederick Sheldon Fellow-
ship.

cal inquiries. Church's summary, however, was limited in two important ways. It did not give specific attention to Eliot's conception of experience as finite center, nor did it attempt to explore the critical possibilities of such a conception.

In his dissertation Eliot had conceived "experience" as "point of view" or, in Bradley's terminology, "finite center." The theory of finite center, he contended, was basic to the whole of Bradley's philosophical system, but somehow it had never received from Bradley vigorous and consistent application: the result was confusion in Bradley's epistemology. The dissertation thus was meant to re-examine problems of knowledge with finite center as its principle of inquiry. It set out to demolish, on the basis of his theory of "point of view" (or "finite center"), the distinction between subject and object (chap. i), between the ideal and the real (chap. ii), and between the "private" and the "public" (chap. iv)—distinctions to which psychologists and metaphysicians like Stout, Alexander, Lipps, Wodehouse, Russell, and Meignon erroneously held in their approaches to the problems of knowledge (chaps. iii, iv, v). In the concluding chapter (chap. vii), Eliot sought to indicate the possibility of a new epistemology constructed on the basis of a theory of "point of view."

Moreover, the dissertation repeatedly refers to "point of view" as a "unity of consciousness." According to Eliot, it is the local configuration of feelings that brings about intelligibility and significance. For him, to analyze the problem of intelligibility and knowledge is to show the modes and aspects of the unification of feelings. The problem of intelligibility, when dialectically conceived as a problem of Unity, yields three closely allied yet distinctive areas of analysis: (1) Unity may be treated as a matter concerning

the permutation of feelings and involving the coincidence
of ideality and reality; (2) it may be taken as a matter concerning the organization of feelings and involving the mutual reference of part and whole; and (3) it may be considered as a matter concerning the degree of perfection
involved in such configuration and transmutation and made
manifest by the range and intensity of the resolution. In
Eliot's critical system, the dialectical principle of Unity appears in turn as principles of Correspondence, Coherence,
and Comprehensiveness. Having based his summary on the
second chapter of the dissertation, which was entitled "On
the Distinction of 'Real' and 'Ideal,' " Church's attention
was completely absorbed by the operation of the principle
of Correspondence in Eliot's theory of knowledge and art.

Lewis Freed in his *T. S. Eliot: Aesthetics and History* had
sensed, at least vaguely, the operation of two of the three
principles in Eliot: namely, the principles of Correspondence and Coherence. He attempted to link Eliot with Aristotle, the Scholastics, Kant, and Bradley. The ancestry of
the dialectic of Unity being so remote (traceable almost to
the very beginning of philosophy itself), and its ramifications in concepts and doctrines being so wide and intricate,
it, indeed, should not be an exaggeration to say that at every
turn in the history of philosophy and criticism one finds
anticipations of Eliot.[29]

Contemporary commentators have not been slow in establishing the critical tradition behind Eliot and in iden-
tifying Eliot's specific obligations in concepts and terms.
Such efforts were first found in the two essays by René
Taupin: "The Example of Rémy de Gourmont," and "The

---

[29] Smidt, *op. cit.*; Grover Smith, Jr., *T. S. Eliot's Poetry and Plays* (Chicago, 1956); and Staffan Bergsten, *Time and Eternity* (Stockholm, 1960),
all suggested long lists of philosophers who might have "influenced" Eliot.

Classicism of T. S. Eliot."[30] Garnet Ree's "A French Influence of T. S. Eliot" compared Eliot, once more, with Gourmont.[31] J. R. Danielles, David Daiches, and Victor Brombert noted T. E. Hulme's influences; G. R. Eliott traced many of Eliot's concepts to Babbitt; M. L. S. Loring related Eliot to Arnold; Mario Praz showed Eliot's obligations to Pound, and Ruth Child observed some similarities between Eliot and Richards.[32] Hugh Kenner and Grover Smith insisted upon the influences of Bradley.[33] John Middleton Murry called Eliot a Neo-Thomist; in A. G. George's opinion, Eliot was rather an Augustinian—one of the variegated progeny of the "Existential" tradition in Christianity.[34] Washington Allston's *Lectures On Art* was considered by one writer as the source of Eliot's "objective correlative"; Whitman's preface to *Leaves of Grass* by another; and, by still another, Husserl's *Logische Untersuchungen* and *Ideen zu einer reiner Phänomenologie unter*

---

[30] René Taupin, "The Example of Rémy de Gourmont," *Criterion*, X (1931), 614; "The Classicism of T. S. Eliot," trans. Louis Zukofsky, *Symposium*, III (1932), 64–84.

[31] Garnet Ree, "A French Influence of T. S. Eliot: Rémy de Gourmont," *Revue de Littérature Comparée* XVI (1936), 764–67.

[32] J. R. Danielles, "T. S. Eliot and His Relation to T. E. Hulme," *The University of Toronto Quarterly*, II (1933), 380–96; David Daiches, "T. S. Eliot and T. E. Hulme," *Poetry and the Modern World* (Chicago, 1940); Victor Brombert, "T. S. Eliot and the Romantic Heresy," *Yale French Studies*, XIII (1954), 3–16; G. R. Eliott, "T. S. Eliot and Irving Babbitt," *The American Review*, VII (1936), 442–54; M. L. S. Loring, "T. S. Eliot on Matthew Arnold," *Sewanee Review*, XLIII (1935), 479–88; Mario Praz, "T. S. Eliot and Dante," *Southern Review*, II (1937), 525–48; Ruth Child, "The Early Critical Work of T. S. Eliot: An Assessment," *College English*, XII (1951), 269–75.

[33] Grover Smith, Jr., "Getting Used to T. S. Eliot," *College English*, XLIX (1960), 1–10, 15; Kenner, *op. cit.*

[34] J. M. Murry, "Towards a Synthesis," *Criterion*, V (1927), 297–313; A. G. George, *T. S. Eliot: His Mind and Art* (Bombay, 1962), esp. pp. 34 ff.; 203 ff.

Phänomenologischen Philosophie.[35] On a larger scale—besides the works of Lewis Freed, A. G. George, and Kristian Smidt—M. F. Moloney attempted to exhibit the combined influences of Arnold, Babbitt, and Hulme; and Edward Greene made a specific study of the French elements in Eliot with particular attention to Baudelaire, Gourmont, Maurras, and Maritain.[36]

But, in the absence of an adequate formulation of Eliot's poetics, the comparisons were in general conducted on a verbal level. Efforts to discover critical principles were often submerged by the enthusiasm for verbal collation.

The purpose of this book is not to outline the dialectical tradition behind Eliot. For such a task, the reformulation of a large number of critical theories (besides Eliot's) would be unavoidable—an enterprise far beyond my scope. Nor does the purpose lie in the affirmation of Eliot's specific obligations in critical concepts and doctrines. My work, in a sense, is a preparation for all that. It aims to restore Eliot's dialectic, so far as it operates in his poetic formulations, in all its main features, and to consider it as a principle of Correspondence as well as of Coherence and Comprehensiveness.

DIALECTIC AS METHOD

In naming Correspondence, Coherence, and Comprehensiveness as the basic features of experience, Eliot finds three

---

[35] Costello, *op. cit.*, p. 66; R. W. Stallman, *The Critic's Notebook* (Minneapolis, 1950), pp. 116, 118; John M. Steadman, "Eliot and Husserl: The Origin of the 'Objective Correlative,'" *Notes and Queries*, CCIII (1958), 261–62. Also cf. McElderly, "Santayana and Eliot's 'Objective Correlative,'" *Boston University Studies in English*, III (1957), 178–81. Eliot in the preface to *Essays on Elizabethan Dramas* (New York, 1957), p. ii, lightly dismissed Allston as a source of his phrase.

[36] M. F. Moloney, "T. S. Eliot and Critical Tradition," *Thought*, XXI (1946), 355–74; Greene, *op. cit.*

lines of analogy for his critical inquiry. In the poetics of Eliot, the resolutions of reality and appearance, of one and many, and of identity and diversity constitute the very grounds on which critical problems are constructed and solved, doctrines proposed and justified. Unity of experience, however, not only stands out as the principle of Eliot's poetic analysis, it also supplies him with a procedure of reasoning. If experience is a continuous process of unification, contradictions and their removal would be in the nature of knowledge. As a method of bringing conflicting elements into relation so that their intelligibility may be exhibited, dialectic is the method for truth.[37] Reflected in the treatment of terms and arguments, the dialectic appears in the doubling and unification of meanings, the opposition and reconciliation of propositions, and the mobility of the "first" principles. "Comparison [reduction] and analysis [distinction]" are the tools with which dialectic operates and which Eliot deems the most basic to criticism. Since each resolution at the moment it is effected immediately generates a new antithesis, it is supposed to be always ready for further resolution into a more comprehensive truth in a hierarchical movement toward Truth. Truth, therefore, is by nature "dynamic." Judgments are provisional and principles are tentative. Eliot contrasts two methods: the method of wis-

---

[37] For the best exposition of the dialectic method, see Richard McKeon, "Philosophy and Method," *Journal of Philosophy*, XLVIII (1951), 653–82. The anonymous article on "Dialectic" in *Syntopicon* (Chicago, 1952) discusses the major types of dialectics; and the article on "Dialectic" by P. Kopnin in *Filosofskaia Entsiklopediia* (1960) (reprinted in *Soviet Studies in Philosophy*, I [1963], 16–22), preoccupied as it is with the Marxist-Leninist dialectic, gives an interesting account of varieties of the dialectic. Herman Sinaiko's *Love, Knowledge, and Discourse in Plato: Dialogue and Dialectic in Phaedrus, Republic, Parmenides* (Chicago, 1965), is indispensable for any one who is interested in Platonic dialectic. Also valuable are R. G. Collingwood, *Essay on Philosophical Method* (Oxford, 1933); Warner Wick, *Metaphysics and the New Logic* (Chicago, 1948).

dom and the method of heresy. Whereas the method of
wisdom recognizes the dynamic process involved in the
search for truth, the heretical method is "fixed" and "one-
sided," taking what is merely a part as a whole, considering
what is merely a stage in the process of knowledge as ultimate, and never looking for common grounds on which the
plurality of truth may be restored to its singularity. In "Civilization: 1928 Model," Eliot treats heresy "as the overem-
phasis of part of truth";[38] in "The Modern Dilemma: Christianity and Communism," he points out that heresy "consists
in emphasizing one aspect of the mystery to the exclusion of
the other."[39] Professor Norman Foerster he names a "heretic" in "Second Thoughts about Humanism" because "Mr.
Foerster [he says] is what I call a Heretic: that is, a person
who seizes upon a truth and pushes it to the point at which
it becomes a falsehood."[40] In *After Strange Gods*, Eliot
concludes: "the essential of any important heresy is not
simply that it is wrong: it is that it is partly right."[41]

Eliot's commentators were fond of talking about his "natural aversion to systems," to which indeed he more than
once confessed.[42] The word system, however, in the works
of Eliot, is an equivocal one and subject to a doubling of

[38] "Civilization: 1928 Model," *Criterion*, VIII (1928), 164.

[39] "The Modern Dilemma: Christianity and Communism," *Listener*,
VII (1932), 382.

[40] *Selected Essays: 1917–1932* (New York, 1932), pp. 399–400. Hereafter
this edition of the *Selected Essays* will be referred to as *SE*.

[41] *After Strange Gods* (London, 1934), p. 26. Also see *The Idea of a
Christian Society* (London, 1939), p. 51: "Heresy is often defined as an
insistence upon one half of the truth; it can also be an attempt to simplify
the truth, by reducing it to the limits of our ordinary understanding,
instead of enlarging our reason to the apprehension of truth."

[42] *For Lancelot Andrewes* (London, 1928), p. 58; *The Use of Poetry
and the Use of Criticism* (London, 1933), p. 150; *The Music of Poetry*
(Glasgow, 1942), p. 42.

senses: one good and one bad. System may mean skeletal abstraction severed from experience or it may refer to the dynamic structure of impressions and feelings. In its bad sense, system is dead scheme; in its good sense, it signifies living order and vital unity. The word systematic, thus, in Eliot's discussion of critics and critical theories, serves as a term of commendation as well as a term of censure. Sometimes he shies away from system. Speaking of Machiavelli, Eliot writes "though he is constructive he is not a system builder, and his thoughts can be repeated but not summarized. It is perhaps a character of his amazing exactness of vision and statement that he should have no 'system'; for a system almost inevitably requires slight distortions and omissions."[43] But on some other occasions, Eliot is most enthusiastic about system. "An impression," he remarks, "needs to be constantly refreshed by new impressions in order that it may persist at all; it needs to take its place in a system of impressions"; and "the perceptions do not, in a truly appreciative mind, accumulate as a mass, but form themselves as a structure."[44]

Eliot's critical theory being a dialectical structure, in one sense, it is most unsystematic; but, in another, it is most systematic. The complaints of Knights, House, Lucas, Bateson, Eastman, Winters, Robbins, Mordell, Austin, and Karl Shapiro are not entirely groundless. All of them, indeed, must be congratulated for having honestly pointed out Eliot's equivocations and contradictions. Their limitation lies in their failure to collect sufficient pairs of conflicting statements so as to discern the characteristic ways in which they are opposed and resolved and the grounds on which such

---

[43] "Niccolò Machiavelli," *For Lancelot Andrewes*, p. 58.
[44] *SW*, pp. 14, 15.

resolution and opposition are justified. This essay aims to exhibit rather than to evaluate Eliot's critical theory. But if any evaluation of Eliot's criticism is to be attempted, it must in the end involve an evaluation of the dialectical method itself.[45]

Indeed, the operation of the dialectic in Eliot had not passed wholly unnoticed among his commentators. After cataloguing eight "critical ideas" in Part I of *The Critical Ideas of T. S. Eliot* (1932) Ants Oras tried to show, in Part II, Eliot's opposition and reconciliation of "individual talent" and "traditional discipline."[46] Leo Shapiro in 1940 noted briefly in Eliot the operation of such Scholastic opposites as essence and existence, potency and act, and conception and creation.[47] Harry Slochower in 1945 mentioned the dialectical resolution of past and present in Eliot: "Eliot brings to issues a dialectical treatment which leads him to consider modernism as an organic part in the final scheme."[48] Charles Moorman in his "Order and Mr. Eliot" (1953) listed "the continual interaction of antagonism" and the operation of the "Coleridgean" principle of "resolution of the opposites" among the basic features of Eliot's method.[49] Seán Lucy in *T. S. Eliot and the Idea of Tradition* (1960) observed: "Eliot's theory of poetry could almost—like the

---

[45] Such criticism may be found in Crane, "Two Essays in Practical Criticism: A Prefatory Note," 199–219; Elder Olson, "Recent Literary Criticism," *Modern Philology*, XL (1943), 275–83; and Richard McKeon, "Rhetoric and Poetic in the Philosophy of Aristotle," *Aristotle's Poetics and English Literature*, ed. Elder Olson (Chicago, 1965), pp. 201–36.

[46] Ants Oras, *The Critical Ideas of T. S. Eliot* (Tartu, 1932), pp. 59 ff.

[47] Leo Shapiro, "The Mediaevalism of Eliot," *Poetry*, LXI (1940), 202–13.

[48] Harry Slochower, *No Voice Is Wholly Lost* (New York, 1945), p. 182.

[49] Charles Moorman, "Order and Mr. Eliot," *South Atlantic Quarterly*, LII (1953), 87.

British constitution—be called a system of checks and bal-
ances."[50]

James Graham, at one point in his dissertation "The Critical Theories of T. S. Eliot and I. A. Richards" (1940),
noted in passing that Eliot's poetic theory was based upon a
theory of reality which assumed the identity of thought and
feeling.[51] But this useful clue was never picked up and vig-
orously pursued. In Eliot's religious formulations the dialectic of reality and appearance produced a series of contrasts
between "Christian feeling" and "Christian thinking," between the conscious formulations ("orthodoxy") and unconscious performances ("tradition"), between dogmas and
the Church, theology and rituals, the mystic and the eccle-
siastic, and so forth; and it led him to censure, on the one
side, the anarchy of Modernism and, on the other, the dog-
matism of Ultramontanism. Failing to grasp Eliot's dialectic,
Graham seized only one side of his arguments. Eliot, according to Graham, identified religion with orthodoxy and
orthodoxy with Roman dogmas. Subscribing to the "intellectual sanction of emotion," Eliot (again according to
Graham) inclined to "intellectualism," "authoritarianism,"
and "mediaevalism" rather than to "voluntarism," "liberal-
ism," and "modernism" as I. A. Richards did.

Like Graham, Leonard Waters in his study "Coleridge
and Eliot" (1948) noted the opposition and resolution of
thought and feeling in Eliot's critical theory.[52] And like
Graham he failed to grasp the full implications of this clue.

---

[50] Seán Lucy, *T. S. Eliot and the Idea of Tradition* (London, 1960), p.
95.

[51] James Graham, "The Critical Theories of T. S. Eliot and I. A.
Richards," (Ph.D. dissertation, University of Wisconsin, 1940).

[52] Leonard Waters, "Coleridge and Eliot: A Comparative Study of
Their Theories of Poetic Composition" (Ph.D. dissertation, University
of Michigan, 1948).

Graham saw only the "medieval" side of Eliot whereas Waters noticed only the "modern" side. Graham labeled Eliot
a dogmatist in religion and a moralist in criticism; Waters,
on the other hand, identified "empirical sciences"—namely,
Freudian psychology and Fraserian anthropology—as the
bases of Eliot's poetics and the French Symbolists and Sur-
realists as the main sources from which Eliot drew his critical concepts. Waters suggested that by virtue of such an
idealizing principle as Imagination, Coleridge was able to
free his poetics from mere emotionalism and objectivism,
and that without such an elevating principle Eliot's poetics
remained "emotive."

The "heretical" treatment of Eliot's poetics (if we may
borrow a word from Eliot himself) is no less prevalent
among those commentators who accepted "personality" or
"impersonality" as the master concept to which all, or at
least a large portion of, Eliot's doctrines are referable. In
Eliot, the opposition between "personality" and "impersonality," in the first place, is a derivation from the opposition
between "particularity" and "universality." The term impersonality is subject to a dialectical doubling: one good
and one bad. In its good sense, impersonality refers to the
universal in the particular, the absolute in its plurality. Good
"impersonality" is found in the poet who "out of intense
and personal experience, is able to express a general truth;
retaining all the particularity of the experience, to make it a
general symbol."[53] In its bad sense, impersonality refers to
generality not sanctioned by particular experiences. "Ordinary education," writes Eliot, "consists largely in the ac-
quisition of *impersonal* ideas which obscure what we really.

---

[53] "A Brief Introduction to the Method of Paul Valéry," *Le Serpent
par Paul Valéry* (London, 1924), p. 13.

are and feel, what we really want, and what really excites our interest."[54] Thus, in the name of "impersonality" Eliot by turns commends and censures poets and artists. Dante and Shakespeare he identifies as true artists and true poets, for they have successfully managed to "transform personal agonies into something impersonal and universal."[55] ("In the greatest poets . . . ," claims Eliot, in "Literature and the Modern World," "private passions are completed in a passionate belief in objective moral values, in a striving towards justice and the life of the spirit among men.")[56] Similarly, Eliot praises Valéry's *Le Serpent* for "like all Valéry's poetry, it is impersonal in the sense that personal emotion, personal experience, is extended and completed in something impersonal."[57] On the other hand, the "impersonal" lyrics of Lovelace, Suckling, and Campion he considers "only craftsman's work" and "anthology pieces," "because one does not feel present in them the particularity which must provide the material for the general truth."[58] "Poetry," says Eliot, "is not a turning loose of emotion, but an escape from emotion; it is not the expression of personality, but an escape from personality. But, of course, only those who have personality and emotions know what it means to want to escape from these things."[59]

The problem of universality in particularity may be formulated, conversely, as a problem of "personality." If good impersonality is found in the revelation of universal significance in particular experience, good personality consists in the individual expression of general truth. As impersonality

54 *SW*, p. 154.   55 *SE*, p. 117.

56 "Literature and the Modern World," *American Prefaces*, I (1935), 21.

57 "Introduction," *Le Serpent*, p. 14.

58 *Ibid.*   59 *SW*, p. 58.

is exposed to the danger of generality, personality may be jeopardized by eccentricity. True personality lies in the enactment of freedom in the tradition of necessity. In his essay "Blake," Eliot commends and reproves Blake by turns for being "personal." Blake enjoys a "naked vision" and a "terrifying honesty" which are essential to poetry, for he has a "personal" point of view. But, on the other hand, just because Blake's point of view is "personal," "naked," and "unregenerated" in the larger whole of impersonal tradition, his poetry remains "provincial," "cranky," and never attains the status of a "classic."[60]

It is, therefore, based upon the contrast and reconciliation of particularity and universality that Eliot talks about "impersonality" and "personality" in poetry. And it is on similar grounds that he speaks of poetry as racial and national, national and international, and so forth.[61] Sometimes he em-

---

[60] "Blake," *SW*, pp. 151–58. See also "The Mysticism of Blake," *Nation and Athenaeum*, XLI (1927), 779, in which a similar argument was advanced: "The [Prophetic] Books are full of poetry, and fine poetry, too. But they show very sadly that genius and inspiration are not enough for a poet. He must have education, by which I do not mean erudition but a kind of mental and moral discipline."

[61] In "A Commentary," *Criterion*, XVII (1937), 82, Eliot observes: "I cannot think of art as either national or international—these, after all are modern terms—but as racial and local; and an art which is not representative of a particular people, but 'international,' or an art which does not represent a particular civilization, but only an abstract civilization-in-general may loose its source of vitality." Again, in "A Commentary," *Criterion*, XIV (1935), 611: "It is not a matter of indifference that poetry written by an Irishman, a Welshman, a Scot, an American or a Jew should be undistinguished." "In his literary nationalism . . . Mr. Yeats," says Eliot (*ibid.*, p. 612), "performed a great service to the English language." In *American Literature and American Language* (St. Louis, 1953), p. 17, he proposes: "Here we arrive at two characteristics which I think must be found together in any author whom I should single out as one of the landmarks of a national literature: the strong local flavour combined with unconscious universality. . . . Cosmopolitanism can be the enemy of universality, it may dissipate attention in superficial familiarity with the streets, the cafés and some of the local dialect of a number of foreign capitals; whereas universality can never come except through writing

phasizes the necessity of particularity; at other times he stresses the importance of universality. "Tradition and the Individual Talent" advocated the "depersonalization" of poetry. But in "T. S. Eliot in Concord" Richard Chase remarked: "He had written *The Waste Land* 'to relieve my emotions,' a purely personal act, Eliot said."[62] Finally the analogy may be slightly adjusted, since whatever is universal may be either as truth and idea are universal or as things and facts are universal. The impersonal poet may be one who expresses general truth in particular symbols or he may be one who records facts and lets them articulate their meanings and significances. Thomas Middleton, Eliot recognizes, is a great poet, for Middleton is a "great recorder," portraying "the individual soul as it is found in a particular phase of society."[63] "There are various degrees of symbolism in imagery," concludes Eliot. "A poet may have a set of imagery come whole and self-sufficient to his mind, so that his sole conscious concern is to set down that vision without concerning himself, in the act of composition, with the meaning of it, but only with the delight of the symmetry of

about what one knows thoroughly." Cf. also "A Letter to the Editor: F. M. Ford," *Transatlantic Review*, I (1924), 95–96.

[62] Richard Chase, "T. S. Eliot in Concord," *American Scholar*, XVI (1947), 442.

[63] "Thomas Middleton," *SE*, pp. 148; "John Ford," *SE*, p. 178. Cf. "Beyle and Balzac," *Athenaeum*, No. 4648 (1919), p. 392: "But Dostoevsky begins with the actual world, as Beyle (Stendhal) does; he only pursues reality farther in a certain direction. In Balzac the fantastic element is of another sort: it is not an extension of reality, it is an atmosphere thrown upon reality direct from the personality of the writer. . . . In the great artist imagination is a very different faculty from Balzac's: it becomes a fine and delicate tool for an operation on the sensible world." Similarly, in the "Preface," *Bubu of Montparnasse* by Charles-Louis Philipe (Paris, 1932), Eliot praises Philipe's "sincerity," a sincerity "which makes him a faithful recorder of things as they are, and of events as they happened, without irrelevant and disturbing comment. He had a gift which is rare enough: the ability not to think, not to generalize."

the picture." On the other hand, there is the kind of poet whose "center of interest [is] not the visible world but in the ceaseless question and answer of the tortured mind."[64]

The dialectic assumes some intricacy in Eliot's treatment of the problem of belief in poetry. Belief, in the critical works of Eliot, has been discussed as the material of art, as the poet's point of view, and as the reader's understanding. Poetry, says Eliot, "is not the assertion that something is true, but the making that truth more fully real to us; it is the creation of a sensuous embodiment."[65] Since poetry consists in the realization of ideas, in any consideration of poetry, inquiry into the technique of realization must be given precedence over inquiry into the material so realized.

---

[64] "Critical Note," *The Collected Poems of Harold Monro* (London, 1933), p. xv. Also cf. Eliot's contrast of Keats with Shelley in *The Use of Poetry and the Use of Criticism*, pp. 87 ff.

[65] "Poetry and Propaganda," *Bookman*, LXX (1930), 601. Also cf. "The Silurist," *Dial*, LXXXIII (1927), 259: "The question whether a poet is a mystic is not, for literary criticism, a question at all. The question is, how far are the poetry and the mysticism one thing? Poetry is mystical when it intends to convey, and succeeds in conveying, to the reader (at the same time that it is real poetry), the statement of a perfectly definite experience which we call the mystical experience." Also, "Introduction," *The Wheel of Fire* by G. Wilson Knight (London, 1930), p. xi: "I have always maintained, not only that Shakespeare was not a philosophical poet in the sense of Dante and Lucretius, but also what may be more easily overlooked, that 'philosophical poets' like Dante and Lucretius are not really philosophers at all. They are poets who have presented us with the emotional and sense equivalent for a definite philosophical system constructed by a philosopher—even though they may sometimes take little liberties with the system." And again in, "Introduction," *All Hallows' Eve* by Charles Williams (New York, 1948), p. xiv: "Chesterton's *The Man Who Was Thursday* is an allegory; it has a meaning which is meant to be discovered at the end; while we enjoy it in reading, simply because of the swiftly moving plot and the periodic surprises, it is intended to convey a definite moral and religious point expressible in intellectual terms. It gives you ideas, rather than feelings, of another world. Williams has no such 'palpable design' upon his reader. His aim is to make you partake of a kind of experience that he has had, rather than to make you accept some dogmatic belief."

I doubt whether belief proper enters into the activity of a great poet, *qua* poet. That is, Dante, *qua* poet, did not believe or disbelieve the Thomist cosmology or theory of the souls; he merely made use of it, or a fusion took place between his initial emotional impulse and a theory, for the purpose of making poetry. The poet makes poetry, the metaphysician makes metaphysics, the bee makes honey, the spider secretes a filament; you can hardly say that any of these agents believes: he merely does.[66]

"From the point of view of art—Christianity was merely a change, a provision of a new world with new material."[67]

But, on the other hand, since "outer unity" is regulated by "inner unity," since the quality of feeling is modified by the quality of thought which supports such feeling, discussions of poetry must take into serious account the quality of belief. "Without doubt," says Eliot in "Dante" (1920):

---

[66] *SE,* p. 118. The poet might be "stimulated" by a philosopher, but production of poetry remains his business, says Eliot in "Shakespeare and Montaigne," *Times Literary Supplement,* No. 1249 (December 24, 1925), p. 895: "Montaigne is just the sort of writer to provide a stimulant to a poet; for what the poet looks for in his reading is not a philosophy—not a body of doctrines or even a consistent point of view which he endeavors to understand—but a point of departure. The attitude of the craftsman like Shakespeare—whose business was to write plays, not to think—is very different from that of the philosopher or even a literary critic."
The conflict between belief and poetry, in a deeper sense, indeed, implicates the perennial conflict between philosophy and art. The problem is solved, in "Shelley and Keats," *The Use of Poetry and the Use of Criticism,* in favor of art. Keats, according to Eliot, in refraining from philosophizing upon his own artistic insight, serves the highest purpose of poetry (and philosophy). Because of his "philosophizing," Shelley is a lesser poet. "I believe," says Eliot (p. 99), "that for a poet to be also a philosopher he would have to be virtually two men; I cannot think of any example of this thorough schizophrenia, nor can I see anything to be gained by it: the work is better performed inside two skulls than one. . . . A poet may borrow a philosophy or he may do without one. It is when he philosophizes upon his own *poetic* insight that he is apt to go wrong."

[67] "A Commentary," *Criterion,* XII (1933), 24.

... the effort of the philosopher proper, the man who is trying to deal with ideas in themselves, and the effort of the poet, who may be trying to *realize* ideas, cannot be carried on at the same time. But this is not to deny that poetry can be in some sense philosophic. The poet can deal with philosophic ideas, not as matter for argument, but as matter for inspection. The original form of a philosophy cannot be poetic. But poetry can be penetrated by a philosophic idea, it can deal with this idea when it has reached the point of immediate acceptance, when it has become almost a physical modification. If we should divorce poetry and philosophy altogether, we should bring a serious impeachment, not only against Dante, but against most of Dante's contemporaries.[68]

"It would be a delusion," Eliot observes in the "Introduction to Goethe" (1929), "to think that we can isolate the poetry of Goethe from his ideas; we cannot understand his feeling without taking his thought seriously."[69] "We can hardly doubt," adds Eliot in "Poetry and Propaganda," "that the 'truest' philosophy is the best material for the greatest poet; so that the poet must be rated in the end by the philosophy he realized in poetry and by the fullness and adequacy of the realization."[70] "Greater philosophy makes greater poetry" because greater philosophy is capable of fuller expansion into artistic vision. "The philosophy which Lucretius tackled," for instance, "was not rich enough in variety of feeling, applied itself to life too uniformly, to

---

[68] *SW*, pp. 162–63. Also see "A Note on Poetry and Belief," *Enemy*, I (1927), 15. Referring to a conversation with I. A. Richards, Eliot writes: "we were agreed, I believe, on one point: that in the history of literature feeling and emotion had been altered, and at certain times diminished, by whatever at the time it was inevitable to consider real and true."

[69] "Introduction to Goethe," *Nation and Athenaeum*, XLIV (1929), 527.

[70] "Poetry and Propaganda," *Literary Opinions in America* (ed. Zabel; New York, 1937), p. 106.

supply the material for a wholly successful poem. It was incapable of complete expansion into pure vision."[71]

Moreover, there are different kinds of poetry. The role of belief in one kind of poetry is not exactly the same as it is in another kind. "The value of Marlowe's verse," says Eliot, "is inseparable from the value of his thought; the value of Milton's verse has no relation to the value of his thought; we may say that the value of Shakespeare's verse transcends and includes the values of his thought."[72] For in poetry of "dissociated sensibility" (Swinburne, Milton) belief is of less importance than in poetry of "unified sensibility." Even among poets of "unified sensibility" a distinction can still be drawn between those who played with ideas for the sake of their emotional values and those who were convinced of the truth of ideas, with feelings coming in as a "by-product."[73]

---

[71] *SW*, p. 162.

[72] "A Study of Marlowe," *Times Literary Supplement*, No. 1309 (1927), p. 140. Characteristically, in *The Use of Poetry and the Use of Criticism*, p. 96, Eliot dichotomizes two extreme types of poets: "I observe in passing that we may distinguish, but without precision, between poets who employ their verbal, rhythmic and imaginative gifts in the service of ideas which they hold passionately, and poets who employ ideas which they hold with more or less settled conviction as material for a poem; poets may vary indefinitely between these two hypothetical extremes, and at what point we place any poet remains incapable of exact calculation."

[73] "Sir John Davies," *On Poetry and Poets* (New York, 1957), p. 154: "Donne was ready to entertain almost any idea, to play with it, to follow it out curiously, to explore all its possibilities of affecting his sensibility. Davies is much more mediaeval; his capacity for belief is greater. He has but the one idea, which he pursues in all seriousness—a kind of seriousness rare in his age. Thought is not exploited for the sake of feeling, it is pursued for its own sake; and the feeling is a kind of by-product, though a by-product worth far more than the thought." The essay was first published in *The Times Literary Supplement* in 1926, the year which saw also the publication of "For Lancelot Andrewes," where occurred Eliot's famous description of the "intensity" of Andrewes' sermon: "When Andrewes begins his sermon, from beginning to end you are sure that he is wholly in his subject, unaware of anything else, that his emotion grows as he penetrates more deeply into his subject, that he is finally 'alone with

The problem may further be formulated in terms of the poet. The interests and activities of a man may be distinguished, but may never be separated from the man himself. A man's interest in philosophy is bound to affect the quality of his art:

> In a sense, indeed, art is dependent upon world outlook; in the sense, namely, that our interest in art cannot be isolated from other interests of life, among them interests of philosophy and religion. But to say that any one type of philosophy is hostile to art or to morals is manifestly unfair; it is truer to say that the type of mind which leans toward one type of philosophy will manifest its peculiarity in its taste in art, and its tastes in morality, as well.[74]

Belief, moreover, is distinguishable into intellectual consent and emotional assent: it may be identified with one's ideas or with one's "point of view," which is "the emotional equivalence of ideas."[75] Whereas ideas properly belong to the domain of philosophy, "point of view" is essentially artistic. The poet should not be burdened with the task of the metaphysician,[76] but a consistent "point of view" is basic to his qualification as a poet. Most devotional poets, remarks Eliot, are guilty of a "pious insincerity," for the beliefs they express are often "held" rather than "felt."[77] Poe, in his

---

the Alone,' with the mystery which he is seeking to grasp more and more firmly. . . . Andrewes' emotion is purely contemplative; it is not personal, it is wholly evoked by the object of contemplation, to which it is adequate; his emotions wholly contained in and explained by its object" (*SE*, p. 299).

[74] "Theism and Humanism," *International Journal of Ethics*, XXVI (1916), 285.

[75] "Kipling Redivivus," *Athenaeum*, No. 4645 (1919), p. 298, claims that Dante, Shakespeare, Villon, and Conrad all "have, in contrast to ideas or concepts, points of view, or 'worlds'—what we incorrectly called 'philosophies.'" For suggestions as to kinds of belief, see *SE*, pp. 218–19.

[76] "Introduction," *Le Serpent*, p. 13.

[77] *After Strange Gods*, p. 30; cf. *The Use of Poetry and the Use of Criticism*, p. 127.

opinion, is an inferior poet because "all his ideas are enter-
tained rather than believed."[78] "I cannot see," says Eliot,
"that poetry can ever be separated from something which I
should call belief, and to which I cannot see any reason for
refusing the name of belief, unless we are to reshuffle names
altogether."[79]

Finally, the problem of belief in poetry may be treated in
relation to the reader. Poetic appreciations, as Eliot says in
From Poe to Valéry (1948), consist in the appreciation of
form and style. In the process of appreciation, three stages
may be discriminated: first, there is the rudimentary enjoyment derived from the subject—"The effect of the poetic
art is felt, without the listener being wholly conscious of the
art." The second stage consists of a "double interest" in the
subject for its own sake and in the way in which it is presented. Lastly, the subject recedes to the background and
becomes a necessary means for the realization of the poem.[80]
If all that is true, belief held in common between the reader
and the poet is not imperative for poetic enjoyment. But
artistic form, in a more profound sense, is derived from the
form of perception a poet imposes upon reality and from
the significance he discerns in reality through such perception. For the more intelligent reader, to appreciate poetry
thus is to understand the poet's point of view—his belief.
There are, Eliot says, "stratifications of public taste": "For
the simplest auditors there is the plot, for the more thought-
ful the character and conflict of character, for the more literary the words and phrasing, for the more musically sensitive the rhythm, and for auditors of greater sensitiveness and
understanding a meaning which reveals itself gradually."[81]

---

[78] *From Poe to Valéry* (New York, 1948), p. 25.

[79] "A Note on Poetry and Belief," *loc. cit.*, p. 16.

[80] *From Poe to Valéry*, p. 25.

[81] *The Use of Poetry and the Use of Criticism*, p. 153.

"Prose writers may be concerned with ideas, but the poet is always concerned with actuality."[82] Since poetry is a concrete object, since it has direct access to the reader's sensibility, a belief common to reader and poet is not necessary for the enjoyment of poetry. But on the other hand, since true appreciation is true understanding and true understanding is not only a matter of sympathy but also a matter of intellect, comprehension of the poet's thought is requisite for the full appreciation of his work. A "mature" and "sane" belief is more easily acceptable than an "adolescent" and "eccentric" one. "If I ask myself (to take a comparison on a higher plane) why I prefer the poetry of Dante to that of Shakespeare, I should have to say, because it seems to me to illustrate a saner attitude towards the mystery of life."[83] Shelley is supposed to be inferior poetically because of the inferiority of his belief.[84]

Since the reader's mind is subject to continuous refinement, the stage of his maturity also would affect his poetic enjoyment. What a reader has passionately admired "at the age of fifteen" may become "unreadable" during his maturer years. To an adolescent reader, " 'The question of belief or disbelief' . . . did not rise."[85] Or, maturation of the reader may affect poetic appreciation in an opposite way. Whatever appears eccentric and alien to a less refined reader may prove tenable for a reader who has mellowed. As his point of view becomes steadily more inclusive, a mature reader may finally overcome and assimilate beliefs which once appeared "strange" and "abominable."[86]

---

[82] *George Herbert* (London, 1962), p. 23.

[83] *SW*, p. x.

[84] *The Use of Poetry and the Use of Criticism*, pp. 97–98.

[85] *Ibid.* p. 97.

[86] "Goethe as the Sage," *On Poetry and Poets* (New York, 1957), pp. 259 ff. This edition of *On Poetry and Poets* will be referred to as *PP* hereafter.

The problem of belief, in its final analysis, is a matter of the quality of belief. True belief is "acceptable" to the audience, "livable" for the poet, and "realizable" in art. In the loftier regions of Eliot's dialectic, analyses of the form of art, the belief of the poet, and the understanding of the audience all can be reduced to analysis of the form of perception and the nature of point of view. To inquire into the role of belief in poetry would ultimately involve inquiries into the nature of reality, truth, and value—inquiries which properly belong to metaphysics. Richards' psychological theory of poetry as "pseudo-statement" Eliot believes to be inadequate, for it asks a supra-scientific question but gives "a merely scientific answer."[87] Limitations of contemporary theories of belief arise, Eliot holds, largely because the theorists fail to see the "supra-scientific" implications of the problem. Without a metaphysical theory to account for the unity in diversity which characterizes human activities, theorists either rigidly adhere to the separation of art and philosophy or attach themselves, with equal rigidity, to their identification.

> The one extreme is to like poetry merely for what it has to say: that is, to like it merely because it voices our own beliefs and prejudices—which is of course to be quite indifferent to the poetry of the poetry. The other extreme is to like the poetry because the poet has manipulated his material into perfect art, which is to be indifferent to the material, and to isolate our enjoyment of poetry from life. The one extreme is not enjoyment of poetry at all, the other is enjoyment of an abstraction which is merely called poetry. But between these extremes occurs a continuous range of appreciations, each of which has its limited validity.[88]

---

[87] "Literature, Science, and Dogma," *Dial*, LXXXII (1927), 241.
[88] "Poetry and Propaganda," *loc. cit.*, p. 103.

DIALECTIC AS A SCHEME OF ACTION

A critical theory which seeks explanation of poetry in the reduction of opposites naturally entails the conclusion that poetic virtue lies in the "balance" of conflicting elements. Moreover, if the dialectic is readjusted, if the rivalry between contraries is construed in historical terms as their alternative predominance in time, effectuation of "balance" would entail a calculus of how to remedy defects and correct excesses in given circumstances. Poetic theory is useful in two ways: it offers a list of fundamental alternatives and it provides a unified scheme of action.[89]

Historians who found in Eliot's "conversion" a development from aestheticism to moralism have committed historical inaccuracies. Eliot's critical essays written before 1928 have unmistakably treated morality as a principle of artistic form, a condition of aesthetic response, and a basis of poetic reality. "The Possibility of a Poetic Drama" (November, 1920), and "Marie Lloyd" (December, 1922), recorded his recognition of common ethos as a condition of aesthetic response whereas "Blake" (February, 1920), argued that true artistic freedom was found in the necessity of orthodoxy and sensibility. Eliot's analysis of the poetry of John Dryden (1922) was no less an analysis of the unity and comprehensiveness of moral vision than his account of

---

[89] A passage in Eliot's "Preface to the English Tradition," *Christendom*, X (1940), 108, in regard to the proper method of social action may be cited here to illustrate this point: "Our first need," writes Eliot, "is always, of course, the Love of God and a Catholic doctrine; the second, to understand the actual situation and the material upon which we have to work; the third, to adapt procedure to the data, and to make the most of what opportunities can be discerned. It is necessary also to have a clear view of the End, of the kind of Society—not as something Utopian, but as something possible in relation to human nature and divine Grace—we want; so that we may at any moment determine our position, and our deflection from the ideal course, by reference to a fixed point."

Dante's art in 1920. In "Philip Massinger" (May, 1920), Eliot takes Massinger's lack of "moral fibre" as the basis for his analysis of the Elizabethan dramatist's form and technique. In "Beyle and Balzac" (May, 1919), Eliot considered Beyle's superiority over Balzac a "moral" superiority.[90] In "Notes on Current Letters" (1922), he declared: "As for the verse of the present time, the lack of curiosity in technical matters of the academic poetry (Georgian, etc.) is only an indication of their lack of curiosity in moral matters."[91] In the "London Letter" which appeared in 1922, Eliot charged:

> The lack of any moral integrity, which I think is behind all the superficial imbecilities of contemporary English verse (imbecilities which an American public is quite able to see for itself) is disguised in various ways; the disguise often takes the form of noble thoughts, and (in serious prose writers also) in endless pomposity. It is the mark of the man who has no core, no individual moral existence, to be possessed with moral notions, to be goaded by the necessity of continual moral formulations.[92]

In the dialectical scheme of Eliot, the distinction between art and morality is by turns sustained and overcome. Art is distinguishable from morality as the expression of value is distinguishable from value itself. On the other hand, since expression derives its characteristics from what is expressed, art is inseparable from morals. Moreover, since art and morals both are modes of activity explainable only in terms of

---

[90] "Beyle and Balzac," *loc. cit.*, pp. 392–93.

[91] "Notes on Current Letters," *Tyro*, I (1922), 4.

[92] "London Letter," *Dial*, LXXII (1922), 512. See also "Mr. Read and M. Fernandez," *Criterion*, IV (1926), 753. The present generation is "a generation which is beginning to turn its attention to an athleticism, a training of the soul as severe and ascetic as the training of the body of a runner."

the universal process of unification, morals bear some artistic features just as art shares many common qualities with morals. In the primitive society, art, morals, and religion are united in one organic "complex."[93] The artist, says Eliot, is more primitive, as well as more civilized, than his contemporaries.[94]

Historians who insisted on Eliot's "conversion" in 1928 failed to treat Eliot's critical theory on its own grounds. They opposed two terms which Eliot's dialectic sought to reconcile as well as to distinguish. Granted that a history of Eliot's development may be constructed with the opposition of art and morals as its basis, such an account should, in all fairness, treat Eliot's "change" as a shifting of emphasis in a unified scheme of action rather than as a sudden mutation or a gradual overcoming of "inconsistencies." The opposition of art and morals, however, is, in one sense, too broad to be useful as a fruitful basis for an account of Eliot's critical development, and in another, too narrow—too broad, since the immediate conditions of art and form can be sought somewhere less remote than morality; too narrow, since morality itself is subject to dialectical manipulations and is explainable, at least, for Eliot, in terms of Unity.

An account of Eliot's development must give adequate attention to Eliot's dialectic of Unity and must describe his change as a shift of emphasis from one end of a dichotomy to the other. This essay aims to discover the unity of Eliot's thought. The next three chapters will devote themselves to the elucidation of Eliot's dialectic of Unity as it operates in his formulations of poetry and criticism; the last chapter will show Eliot's change in doctrines as relative to a unified

---

[93] *Notes towards a Definition of Culture* (London, 1948), p. 29.

[94] "War Paint and Feathers," *Athenaeum*, No. 4668 (1919), p. 1036.

scheme of action. It proposes that Eliot's earlier doctrines were designed to advocate the poetry of "concentration" whereas his later doctrines pleaded for the poetry of "expansion." Concentration and expansion are terms indicative of the two basic directions of movement involved in a theory of Unity—the centripetal and the centrifugal; meanwhile they are specific enough to render intelligible the nature of Eliot's change in critical doctrines.

The Conditions of Art

TRANSMUTATION

Eliot's dialectic manifests itself differently as different critical principles when different moments or aspects of Unity are emphasized. When attention is directed to the transmutation of appearance into reality (or, vice versa, to the embodiment of reality in appearance), the principle of Correspondence emerges. When attention is directed to the integration of parts into a whole (or vice versa, to the manifestation of the whole through its parts), the principle of Coherence appears. And, finally, when attention is given to the identification of the opposites (or, vice versa, to the contradiction of the likes), the principle of Comprehensiveness enters.

In Eliot's critical discussions, Comprehensiveness, Coherence, and Correspondence constantly operate as the grounds for distinction and reduction, for analysis and integration, and for refutation and restatement. Through the proliferation of propositions couched in numerous equivalents and covariables of such basic dichotomies as reality and appearance, one and many, and identity and difference, this triad of critical principles generates a vast body of doctrines and tenets, ready to be employed in the determination of the requirements and qualifications of the poet (chap. iii), in the diagnosis of conditions and circumstances conducive to the production of various kinds of poetry (chap. iii), and in the elucidation and evaluation of the poetic art (chap. ii).

The art of poetry Eliot takes, in the first place, as an art of "transmutation" involved in the construction of the "semblance" of "reality," the "statement" of "truth," and the "expression" of "meaning." To indicate the two basic, yet opposed, ingredients involved in the art of transmutation, Eliot appeals to two sets of terms: one includes synonyms for and equivalents of what may be called "reality" (which is identifiable by its intelligibility), and the other consists of cognates and derivatives of what may be called "appearance" (which is knowable by its tangibility). Thus, in his "Introduction" to *The Wheel of Fire* (1930), Eliot suggests that "in a work of art, as truly as anywhere, reality only exists in and through appearance. . . . Poetry is poetry, and the surface is as marvellous as the core."[1] Thus, in "A Note on War Poetry" (1942), Eliot indicates that poetry is the symbol generated out of the meeting of Spirit and Nature.[2] In a review of Yeats's letters (1917), he remarks that poetry is truth seen in passion.[3] In "Goethe as the Sage" (1955), he considers poetry as a convergence of "wisdom" and "poetic speech"; in "Shakespeare and the Stoicism of Seneca," (1927), he takes poetry as the confluence of "permanent human impulse" and "perfect language." "Dante as a 'Spiritual Leader'" (1920) pairs off ideas with facts; "Tradition and the Individual Talent" (1919) couples significance with emotion.

---

1 "Introduction," *The Wheel of Fire*, p. xix.

2 "A Note on War Poetry," *London Calling*, ed. Storm Jameson (New York, 1942), pp. 237–38. Reprinted in *Collected Poems: 1909–1962* (London, 1963).

3 "The Letters of J. B. Yeats," *Egoist*, IV (1917), 89.

Since transmutation at once involves the idealization of appearance and the objectification of reality, the poetic process easily lends itself to twofold description. Sometimes Eliot treats poetry as an art of "incarnation," "embodiment," "realization," and "presentation"; and, at other times, he considers it an effort, on the part of objects and feelings, toward intellectual "formulation" and significant "articulation"—"Every precise emotion tends towards intellectual formulation."[4] Be it treated as the idealization of things and objects, or, conversely, as the presentation of ideas and thoughts, the art of poetry, for Eliot, remains the art of transmutation. Art, says he, never improves; only the materials of art change.[5]

Eliot's concept of art as Correspondence receives some refinement when, instead of analyzing poetry in terms of one inclusive contrast between reality and appearance, he begins to introduce three pairs of more particularized opposites and to couch his poetic discussion in three movements by successively treating poetry as the "emotional equivalence of thought," as the "objective equivalence" of significant emotion, and as the "verbal equivalent" of thought, emotion, and action.

When poetry is considered "the emotional equivalent of thought," the unification of thought and emotion is said to be basic to the poetic art. The Metaphysical poets, Eliot indicates, excelled in this art of union.

> Of Metaphysical poetry in general, [observes Eliot] we may say that it gets its effects by suddenly producing an emotional equivalent for what seemed merely a dry idea, and by finding the idea a vivid emotion. It moves between

---

[4] "Shakespeare and the Stoicism of Seneca," *SE*, p. 115.

[5] "Tradition and the Individual Talent," *SE*, p. 6: ". . . art never improves, but the material of art is never quite the same."

abstract thought and concrete feeling; and strikes us largely by contrast and continuity, by the curious ways in which it shows thought and feeling as different aspects of one reality.[6]

"The usual course for Donne," adds Eliot in *A Garland for John Donne* (1931), "is not to pursue the meaning of the ideas but to arrest it, to play cat-like with it, to develop it dialectically, to extract every minimum of the emotion suspended in it."[7] And, in "Views and Reviews" (1935) he continues, "We usually get either a frigid philosophical dexterity, or an emotional slop; whereas in the Carolines, in general, intellectual acuteness and warm feeling are equally united."[8]

Union of thought and feeling may be achieved by what Eliot has called the "metaphysical" method: "Donne was ready to entertain almost any idea, to play with it, to follow it out of curiosity, to explore all its possibilities of affecting his sensibility."[9] Opposed to the "metaphysical" method, there is, however, what Eliot has called the "philosophical" method, of which Sir John Davies, we are told, is a master.

Davies is much more mediaeval; his capacity for belief is greater. He has but one idea, which he pursues in all seriousness. . . . Thought is not exploited for the sake of feeling, it is pursued for its own sake; and the feeling is a kind of by-product, though a by-product worth far more than thought.[10]

---

[6] "Rhyme and Reason: The Poetry of John Donne," *Listener*, III (1930), 502.

[7] "Donne in Our Time," *A Garland for John Donne*, ed. T. Spencer (Cambridge, Mass., 1931), pp. 12–13.

[8] "Views and Reviews III," *New English Weekly*, VII (1935), 190.

[9] "Sir John Davies," *loc. cit.*, p. 154. This essay first appeared in *The Times Literary Supplement* in 1926. It was not listed in Gallup, *op. cit.*

[10] "Sir John Davies," *loc. cit.*, p. 157.

The distinction, which Eliot had proposed in "Sir John
Davies" (1926), was maintained in "Rhyme and Reason"
(1930), where the "metaphysical" method of Donne was
contrasted with the "philosophical" method of Dante: "In
philosophical poetry the poet *believes* in some theory about
life and the universe and makes poetry of it. Metaphysical
poetry, on the other hand, does not imply belief; it has come
to mean poetry in which the poet *makes use of* metaphysical
ideas and theories."[11] Whichever method the poet uses to
achieve the union, poetry, for Eliot, remains the art involved
in the "re-creation of thought into feeling"; and the poet is
one who "has that strange gift, so rarely bestowed, for turning thought into feeling."[12]

The concept of poetry as "the emotional equivalent of
thought" not only enables Eliot to distinguish "philosophical" poetry from "metaphysical" poetry and thereby to
identify the two "hypothetical extremes" of poetic method;
it also provides grounds for him to separate "artistic emotion" from "floating sentiment" and to distinguish "abstract
ideas" from poetic truth, and thereby to condemn poetry in
which intellect is "unsanctioned" by emotion alongside
poetry in which emotion is "unsanctioned" by intellect.
Eliot contrasts Tennyson with Donne; the former he considers a "reflective" poet and the latter, an "intellectual"
one: "Tennyson and Browning are poets, and they think;
but they do not feel their thought as immediately as the
odour of a rose. A thought to Donne was an experience; it
modified his sensibility."[13] Disjuncture of thought and feeling yields, on the one side, sensationalism; and, on the other,

---

[11] "Rhyme and Reason: The Poetry of John Donne," *loc. cit.*, p. 502.
[12] "Sir John Davies," *loc. cit.*, p. 153.
[13] "The Metaphysical Poets," *SE*, p. 247.

didacticism. Dryden, Eliot observes, "bears a curious anti-
thetical resemblance to Swinburne."[14] Sentimentalism and
intellectualism sometimes are found simultaneously in the
works of one single poet. "In Laforgue," says Eliot, "there
are unassimilated fragments of metaphysics, and, on the other
hand, of sentiment floating about."[15] The concept of poetry
as "the emotional equivalence of thought," furthermore,
affords Eliot apparatus to compare poetry that exhibits
"unified sensibility" but is "predominated" by one element
or another. Among the Metaphysical poets, for instance,
Herbert's poetry is predominated by sensibility and Donne's
by intellect. The poetry of Donne is the poetry of "wit,"
whereas Herbert's is the poetry of "magic."[16]

When Eliot adopts the thought-emotion contrast to frame
his poetic discussion, the "fusion" of thought and feeling
appears to be the determinant of poetic excellence. The discussion, however, may be shifted to the verbal level. Once
Eliot chooses the verbal approach and places his critical
analysis within the framework of the contrasting pair of
sound and sense, "coöperation" between sound and sense
becomes basic. Eliot distinguishes three parts of the word:
sound, imagery, and meaning.[17] He sometimes allies imagery
with meaning and investigates the nature of poetry in terms
of the sound-sense dichotomy. At other times he collapses
meaning with sound and uses the object-word contrast to
state his critical problem. "Language in a healthy state," says
Eliot, "presents the object, is so close to the object that the
two are identified; . . . the bad poet dwells partly in a world

---

14 "John Dryden," *SE*, p. 273.

15 "Observations," *Egoist*, V (1918), 69.

16 *George Herbert*, p. 18.

17 *Ezra Pound, His Metric and Poetry* (New York, 1917), p. 14.

of objects and partly in a world of words, and he never can get them to fit."[18] "The music of poetry is not something which exists apart from the meaning," *The Music of Poetry* comments.[19] And, "for poetry to approach the condition of music . . . it is not necessary that poetry should be destitute of meaning."[20] "Poetry of different kinds," concludes Eliot, "may be said to range from that in which the attention of the reader is directed primarily to the sound, to that in which it is directed primarily to the sense. . . . But with either type sound and sense must coöperate."[21]

Eliot's analysis of the consequences of linguistic disjuncture falls well in line with his dialectical scheme. "Milton," says he, "in exploring the orchestral music of language, sometimes ceases to talk a social idiom at all. Wordsworth, in attempting to recover the social idiom, sometimes oversteps the mark and becomes pedestrian."[22] On the one hand, the vices of "colloquial jargon"; on the other, "morbidity" of language. Indeed, Milton, Swinburne, and Poe are all supposed to be conspicuous instances of linguistic decadence. "Milton," charges Eliot, "adopts a tortuous style, the involved style of Latin, which is dictated by the demand of verbal music, instead of the demand of sense."[23] No less severe is Eliot's criticism of Swinburne. In *Ezra Pound, His Metric and Poetry*, he indicates that Swinburne's adjectives

---

[18] "Swinburne as Poet," *SW*, p. 149.

[19] "The Music of Poetry," *PP*, p. 21.

[20] *Ezra Pound, His Metric and Poetry*, p. 13.

[21] *From Poe to Valéry*, p. 14.

[22] "The Music of Poetry," *PP*, p. 29.

[23] "A Note on the Verse of Milton," *Essays and Studies by Members of the English Association*, XXI (ed. Herbert Read; Oxford, 1936), 35. Statement was modified when it reappeared in "Milton I," *PP*, p. 161.

are "blanks."[24] In "Swinburne as Poet," he complains that Swinburne dwells "exclusively" in the world of words. "Isolated Superiority" charges that "Swinburne's form is uninteresting, because he is literally saying next to nothing."[25] And "Kipling Redivivus" labels Swinburne a vicious rhetorician.

> Swinburne and Mr. Kipling have, like the public speaker, an idea to impose; and they impose it in the public speaker's way, by turning the idea into sound, and iterating the sound. And, like the public speaker's, their business is not to express, to lay before you, to *state*, but to propel, to impose on you the idea.[26]

Morbidity of language Eliot also finds to be the weakness of Poe. Poe, we are told, "has an incantatory element, . . . in his choice of the word which has the right sound, Poe is by no means careful that it should also have the right sense."[27] Hopkins, Massinger, Beaumont, and Fletcher afford more instances of verbal decadence. "The evocative quality of the verse of Beaumont and Fletcher," says Eliot, "depends upon a clever appeal to emotions and associations which they have not themselves grasped, it is hollow."[28] Massinger's "feeling for language has outstripped his feeling for things"; "his eye and his vocabulary were not in co-operation."[29] And "Hopkins' innovations come near to being purely verbal."[30]

Discussion of poetic unity takes another turn when Eliot

---

[24] *Ezra Pound, His Metric and Poetry*, p. 13.

[25] "Isolated Superiority," *Dial*, LXXXIV (1928), 6.

[26] "Kipling Redivivus," *loc. cit.*, p. 297.

[27] *From Poe to Valéry*, p. 13.

[28] "Ben Jonson," *SE*, p. 135.

[29] "Philip Massinger," *SE*, p. 185.

[30] *After Strange Gods*, p. 51.

introduces the prose-poetry contrast. "We seem to see
clearly enough," remarks Eliot, "that prose is allowed to be
'poetic'; we appear to have overlooked the right of poetry to
be 'prosaic.' "[31] "Prose which has nothing in common with
poetry is dead; whereas verse which has nothing in common with prose is probably artificial, false, diffuse, and syn-
tactically weak."[32] The verse of Goldsmith and Johnson is
poetry, Eliot insists, "partly because it has the virtues of
good prose."[33]

Eliot's well-known paradox (which he borrowed from
Pound, who in turn had borrowed from Ford Madox
Hueffer)—"Poetry must be as well written as prose"—
much discussed as it is, really amounts to nothing more than
a reaffirmation of the unity of language in what he construes
to be a period of verbal decadence.[34] "Every revolution in
poetry," observes Eliot, "is apt to be, and sometimes an-
nounces itself to be, a return to common speech."[35]

Eliot admires Dryden, for Dryden, in his opinion, did try
to rescue the English language from decadence: "What
Dryden did in fact was to reform the language, and devise
a natural, conversational style of speech in verse in place of
an artificial and decadent one."[36]

Between the two extremes of *incantation* and *meaning* we
are I think today more easily seduced by the music of

---

[31] "Prose and Verse," *loc. cit.*, p. 5.

[32] *John Dryden: The Poet, the Dramatist, the Critic* (New York, 1932),
p. 44.

[33] "Johnson's *London* and *The Vanity of Human Wishes*," *English
Critical Essays: Twentieth Century,* ed. Phyllis M. Jones (London, 1933),
p. 304.

[34] *The Use of Poetry and the Use of Criticism,* p. 152; "Introduction,"
Selected Poems by Marianne Moore (New York, 1935), p. ix.

[35] "The Music of Poetry," *loc. cit.*, p. 23.

[36] *John Dryden,* p. 10.

the exhilaratingly meaningless, than contented with intelligence and wisdom set forth in pedestrian measures.
The age of Johnson, and Johnson himself, were more in-
cline to the latter choice. . . . We forgive much to sound
and image, he forgave much to sense.[37]

Since poetry does periodically suffer from "pedestrian"
idiom, to explore the musical possibilities of language is as
much a task of the poet as the adaptation of verse to colloquial speech. "Poetry," Eliot remarks, "may occur . . . at
any point along a line of which the formal limits are 'verse'
and 'prose.' "[38]

Once verse is brought forth as a medium of poetry, problems regarding the coöperation between sound and sense return as problems of the correspondence of rhythm to the
content, the adequacy of outer form to the inner form, and
the possibility of free verse, and so forth. "To create a
form," writes Eliot, "is not merely to invent a shape, a
rhyme, or rhythm. It is also the realization of the whole
appropriate content of this rhyme or rhythm."[39] The outer
form, in other words, must be completely adequate to the
inner form. Verse cannot be free because it never can be
"liberated" from form. But, on the other hand, since form
changes with the change of sensibility, verse may have to
free itself from "set forms" which are no longer appropriate
to the new content. The free verse movement, Eliot argues,
should be construed as a departure from dead forms rather
than as a revolt against form.[40]

37 "Johnson as Critic and Poet," *PP*, p. 193.

38 "Preface," *Anabasis: A Poem by St. J. Perse* (New York, 1938), p. 9.

39 "The Possibility of a Poetic Drama," *SW*, p. 63.

40 "Reflections on *Vers Libre*," *New Statesman*, VIII (1917), 518–19;
for other discussions of free verse, see also "The Music of Poetry," *loc.
cit.*, pp. 31–32, and *Ezra Pound: His Metric and Poetry*, p. 10.

The artist of subtler genius, Eliot observes, makes his art by "feeling and contemplating feelings"; the more masculine kind, however, relies upon some objective tokens for the expression of feelings and emotions.[41] The artistic use of "objective correlative" is warranted by human nature, for "it is universally human to attach the strongest emotions to definite tokens."[42] "Permanent literature," Eliot further explains in "The Possibility of a Poetic Drama," "is always a presentation: either a presentation of thought, or a presentation of feeling by a statement of events in human action or objects in the external world."[43] "Hamlet and His Problems" adds:

> The only way of expressing emotion in the form of art is by finding an "objective correlative"; in other words, a set of objects, a situation, a chain of events which shall be the formula of that particular emotion; such that when the external facts, which must terminate in sensory experience, are given, the emotion is immediately evoked.[44]

Once Eliot turns his attention to the objective correlative, the principle of Correspondence reappears as the doctrine of "doubleness in action." "It is possible," says Eliot, "that what distinguishes poetic drama from the realistic drama is a kind of doubleness in action, as if it took place on two planes at once."[45] "A verse play," he proposes, "is not a play done in verse, but a different kind of play; in a way more real than the 'naturalistic' drama, because instead of clothing nature in poetry, it should remove the surface of things,

---

41 "London Letter," *Dial*, LXXI (1921), 216.

42 "Reflections on Contemporary Poetry I," *Egoist*, IV (1917), 118.

43 "The Possibility of a Poetic Drama," *loc. cit.*, pp. 64–65.

44 "Hamlet and His Problems," *SW*, p. 100.

45 "John Marston," *Elizabethan Essays* (London, 1934), p. 189.

expose the underneath, or the inside, or the natural surface."[46]

In his verbal approach to poetry, Eliot suggests "verse"
and "prose" as the two hypothetical "limits" of poetic form;
in his objective approach he proposes "liturgy" and "realism" as the "termini" of poetic action. "Dramatic form,"
writes Eliot, "may occur at various points the termini of
which are liturgy and realism; at one extreme the arrow-
dance of the Todas and at the other Sir Arthur Pinero. . . .
In genuine drama the form is determined by the point on
the line at which a tension between liturgy and realism takes
place."[47]

Whereas "liturgy" is supposed to offer maximum meaning with minimum detail, "realism" presents details with
minimum significance. To the Eliot of the Selected Essays
liturgical art evidently is the preferred art. It is simply because of this preoccupation that Eliot, in "A Dialogue on
Dramatic Poetry," speaks of the Mass as the "highest kind
of poetry"; and, in his review of Poems and Marriage, holds
that "all art emulates the condition of ritual."[48] It is because
of this preoccupation that Eliot praises Marlowe's art of
"caricature," admires Jonson's "farce," and accords poetic
superiority to the symbolic Baudelaire rather than to the
documentary Huysmans.[49] Also in this connection, Eliot de-
plores, in "Four Elizabethan Dramatists," the "artistic
greediness" of Webster, Tourneur, Middleton, and Chapman.[50] "It is essential," affirms Eliot,

[46] "Introduction," Shakespeare and the Popular Dramatic Tradition by
S. L. Bethell (Westminster, 1943), p. 8.

[47] "Introduction," Savonarola by Charlotte Eliot (London, 1926), p. x.

[48] "Marianne Moore," Dial, LXXV (1923), p. 597.

[49] "Ben Jonson," SE, pp. 127 ff.; "Baudelaire," SE, p. 342.

[50] "Four Elizabethan Dramatists," SE, pp. 91 ff.

that a work of art should be self-consistent, that an artist should consciously or unconsciously draw a circle beyond which he does not trespass: on the one hand, actual life is always the material, and on the other hand, an abstraction from life is a necessary condition to the creation of the work of art.[51]

The four Elizabethan dramatists, according to Eliot, have patently failed to draw a right "circle"—to postulate and establish rules of dramatic conventions that would have helped them keep out superfluous details. They are not "abstract" enough because they have failed to make the proper use of conventions. Conventions thus do serve artistic purposes. Eliot likens the art of poetry to the art of ballet, for both are "formal" and both rely upon some established conventions to exclude realistic elements.[52]

> In the ballet only that is left to the actor which is properly the actor's part. The general movements are set for him. There are only limited movements that he can make, only a limited degree of emotion that he can express. He is not called upon for his personality. The difference between a great dancer and a merely competent dancer is in the vital flame, that impersonal, and if you like, inhuman force which transpires between each of the great dancer's movements. So it would be in a strict form of drama; but in realistic drama, which is drama striving steadily to escape the conditions of art, the human being intrudes.[53]

---

[51] *Ibid.*, p. 93.

[52] *Religious Drama: Mediaeval and Modern* (New York, 1954), p. 15. Cf. Valéry's prose: poetry::walking: dancing ("Introduction," *The Art of Poetry* by Paul Valéry, p. xv).

[53] "Four Elizabethan Dramatists," *loc. cit.*, p. 95. Cf. "London Letter," *Dial*, LXXI (1921), p. 214: M. Diaghileff's "ballet is more sophiticated but also more simplified, and simplifies more; and what is needed of art is a simplification of current life into something rich and strange. This simplification neither Congreve nor Mr. Shaw attained; and however brilliant their comedies, they are a divagation from art." Also see "Dramatis Personae," *Criterion*, I (1923), 303–6; "The Ballet," *Criterion*, III (1925), 441–43.

Eliot's poetic drama is distinguishable, on the one hand, from realistic drama, which is not "abstract" enough, and, on the other, from the "drama of ideas," which is not "real" enough. Goethe's *Faust* Eliot believes to be artistically defective. For "Goethe's demon inevitably sends us back to Goethe. He embodies a philosophy. A creation of art should not do that: he should *replace* the philosophy. Goethe has not, that is to say, sacrificed or consecrated his thought to make the drama; the drama is still the means."[54] Eliot exempts *The Dynasts* from the camp of drama of ideas. "This gigantic panorama," comments he, "is hardly to be called a success, but it is essentially an attempt to present a vision, and 'sacrifices' the philosophy to the vision, as all great dramas do. Mr. Hardy has apprehended his matter as a poet and an artist."[55]

In Eliot's dialectical scheme, the unity of sound and sense, of action and philosophy, and of thought and emotion, all have a narrower application as well as a broader one. In their restricted application, they are merely extensions and variations of the form-and-matter formulation. The verbal equivalent is form to the objective correlative as the objective correlative to the emotional equivalent, which, being a "fusion" of thought and emotion, can be indifferently called either thought or emotion. Action, it may be said, expresses emotions and ideas. But in the loftier areas of discussion, Eliot's concept of "doubleness of action" is a variation of his concept of the dual nature of reality (which Bradley had elaborated in *Appearance and Reality* and which Eliot himself wrestled with in his doctoral dissertation). Action and character in a poetic drama are supposed to have a natural-

---

[54] "The Possibility of a Poetic Drama," *loc. cit.*, p. 66.

[55] *Ibid.*, p. 66 n.

istic reality and a spiritual reality as well. In a play, the spiritual meaning is given concrete evidence as realistic details are elevated by the universal truth they embody. Thus Eliot argues in "Thomas Heywood" that Heywood had been "misleadingly" called a realist. For "behind the motion of his personages, the shadow of the human world, there is no moral synthesis; to inform the verse there is no vision."[56] On the other hand, Eliot considers Marston a true poet. For Marston succeeds, at least in *Sophonisba*, to exhibit

> a pattern behind pattern into which the characters deliberately involve themselves; the kind of pattern which we perceive in our lives only at rare moments of inattention and detachment, drowsing in sunlight. It is the pattern drawn by what the ancient world called Fate; subtilized by Christianity into mazes of delicate theology; and reduced again by the modern world into crudities of psychological or economic necessity.[57]

Considerations on planes of reality in dramatic action and character lead to Eliot's multifarious distinctions between the ethical and the sentimental, the tragic and the pathetic, and the theatrical and the symbolical. In "Thomas Heywood" Eliot describes the plots of *A Woman Killed with Kindness* and *The English Traveller* as pathetic rather than tragic. "Mrs. Frankford," writes Eliot, "yields to her seducer with hardly a struggle, and her decline and death are a tribute to popular sentiment; not, certainly, a vindication of inexorable moral law."[58] Again, "for a Corneille or Racine, the center of interest in the situation of Mrs. Frankford or Mrs. Wincott would have been the moral conflict

---

[56] "Thomas Heywood," *SE*, p. 152.

[57] "John Marston," *Elizabethan Essays*, p. 194.

[58] "Thomas Heywood," *loc. cit.*, p. 157.

leading up to the fall; and even the absence of conflict, as in the seduction of Mathilde (if seduction it can be called) in *Le Rouge et le Noir*, can be treated by a moralist."[59] Action and character in Heywood, Eliot concludes, are real only on the sentimental level: "Heywood's is a drama of common life, not, in the highest sense, tragedy at all; there is no supernatural music from behind the wings. He would in any age have been a successful playwright; he is eminent in the pathetic, rather than the tragic."[60]

In "John Ford," Eliot contrasts Ford's theatrical treatment of dramatic recognition with Shakespeare's symbolic treatment. In Shakespeare's plays, says Eliot, recognition

> is primarily the recognition of a long-lost daughter, secondarily of a wife; and we can hardly read the later plays attentively without admitting that the father and daughter theme was one of very deep symbolic value to him in his last productive years: Perdita, Marina and Miranda share some beauty of which his earlier heroines do not possess the secret. Now Ford is struck by the dramatic and poetic effectiveness of the situation, and uses it on a level hardly higher than that of the device of twins in comedy; so in *The Lover's Melancholy* he introduces two such scenes, one the recognition of Eroclea in the guise of Parthenophil by her lover Palador, the second her recognition . . . by her aged father Meleander. . . . The scenes, as said above, are well planned and well written, and are even moving; but it is in such scenes as these that we are convinced of the incommensurability of writers like Ford (and Beaumont and Fletcher) with Shakespeare. . . . In their poetry there is no symbolic value; theirs is good poetry and good drama, but it is poetry and drama of the surface.[61]

---

[59] *Ibid.*

[60] *Ibid.*, p. 158.

[61] "John Ford," *SE*, pp. 171–72.

ORGANIZATION

Eliot's treatment of poetry as the "emotional co-efficient,"
the "objective correlative," and the "verbal token" furnishes grounds for his division of the main types of poetry
and poetic method. Poetry, we are told, ranges from prose to
verse, from realism to liturgy, and from the "metaphysical"
play with emotions to the "philosophical" contemplation of
ideas. In poetry, coöperation and interplay between
thought, emotion, action, and words are supposed to be
constantly maintained; and the balance and fusion, the harmony and tension, between the poetic elements produce
poetic "intensity." As intensity is the mark of genuine
poetry, so the lack of it yields six kinds of poetic perversion:
verbalism, colloquialism, naturalism, didacticism, sensationalism, and abstractivism. On the other hand, Eliot's scheme
allows for unlimited poetic classifications. Since the degree
of harmony and tension between poetic elements varies, and
since poetic intensity is likewise subject to innumerable
gradations, the classification of poetic kinds and poetic
methods is an endless task.

Eliot's analysis of poetry is further complicated by the
introduction of the principle of Coherence. His concept of
poetry radically changes, and a new cluster of terms and
definitions appears once he shifts the basis of critical inquiry
from considerations of Unity as Correspondence to considerations of Unity as Coherence. In the new context, the
problem in question is now a problem concerning the unification of parts into the whole rather than the problem related to the interdependence of thought, passion, action, and
words. Distinctions among kinds of organization (contextual, aggregative, and so forth) replace distinctions among
types of reality (abstract, realistic, poetic). And terms re-

lated to order, structure, design, and pattern now come into new prominence. The term "form," formerly synonymous with "vehicle of expression," now is given a new signification, serving as an equivalent of "order" and "structure." "A degree of heterogeneity of material," says Eliot, "compelled into unity by the operation of the poet's mind is omnipresent in poetry."[62] And John Livingston Lowes, observes Eliot, owes his distinction as a critic to his convincing demonstration, in *The Road to Xanadu*, "that poetic originality is largely an original way of assembling the most disparate and unlikely material to make a new whole."[63]

The selection of diction and the contrivance of plot, which, in the context of Correspondence, would be problems related to the choice of "word flesh" and the adoption of "material token," now with the shift of the ground of argument from Correspondence to Coherence, all become problems of "pattern," "design," and "structure." Art is now conceived as an art of organization rather than an art of transmutation. Each word, Eliot suggests, is a very complex musical structure, and "there is an implicit unity between all meanings of a word."[64] The creation of a "pattern" of meanings is what the poet aims at and the poetic art consists of.

> To find the word and give it the utmost meaning, in its place; to mean as many things as possible, to make it both exact and comprehensive, and really to unite the disparate and remote, to give them a fusion and a pattern within the word, surely this is the mastery at which the poet aims.[65]

---

[62] "The Metaphysical Poets," *loc. cit.*, p. 243.

[63] "The Frontiers of Criticism," *PP*, p. 119.

[64] "The Aims of Education 1," *loc. cit.*, p. 8.

[65] "Preface," *Transit of Venus: Poems by Harry Crosby* (Paris, 1931), p. viii.

What is true of a single word is, a fortiori, true of a poem. The mastery at which the poet always aims is the construction of a very complex musical structure.

Eliot broadly distinguishes two types of poetic music: (1) the simple melodious verse which yields the music of sound; and (2) the complex verbal organization which is the music of meaning re-enforced by the music of sound. *Ezra Pound, His Metric and Poetry* contrasts the music of Swinburne with the music of Pound: the music of Pound, says Eliot,

> is very different from what is called the "music" of Shelley or Swinburne, a music often nearer to rhetoric (or the art of the orator) than to the instrument. . . . For poetry to approach the condition of music . . . it is not necessary that poetry should be destitute of meaning. Instead of the slightly veiled and resonant abstractions . . . of Swinburne, or the mossiness of Mallarmé, Pound's verse is always definite and concrete, because he has always a definite emotion behind it.[66]

"Thinking in Verse" (1930) opposes the verse of Campion to the verse of Donne:

> There are two kinds of "music" in verse. . . . The song of Campion is as simple in content as possible; its merit lies in its delicate, irregular metre responsive to the music. Donne's lyric has a similar skilful irregularity; but the metrical beauty is so closely associated with the thought, that if it were sung, the sense would be lost. And Donne's is the second kind of musical verse: the verse which suggests music, but which, so to speak, contains in itself all its possible music; for if set to music, the play of ideas could not be followed.[67]

"The Music of Poetry" (1942) summarizes: "A 'musical poem' is a poem which has a musical pattern of sound and a

---

[66] *Ezra Pound, His Metric and Poetry*, p. 13.
[67] "Thinking in Verse," *Listener*, III (1930), 441.

musical pattern of the secondary meanings of the words
which compose it, and that these two patterns are indis-
soluble and one."[68] And,

> the music of a word is, so to speak, at a point of inter-
> section: it arises from its relation first to the words im-
> mediately preceding and following it, and indefinitely to
> the rest of its context; and from another relation, that of
> its immediate meaning in that context to all the other
> meanings which it has had in other contexts, to its greater
> or less wealth of association.[69]

A poem is more "musical" and therefore more poetic when
it commands greater contextual refinement and better organization.

No less a problem of structure and order is the contrivance of the "objective correlative." The doctrine of three
unities Eliot considers useful but inadequate: useful, since
the doctrine recognizes that unity generates poetic intensity;[70] inadequate, since unity of time and unity of place are
only instrumental to the unity of action, which, in turn, is
instrumental to and conditioned by what Eliot has variously
called "the unity of inspiration," "the unity of feeling," "the
unity of sentiment," and "emotional unity."[71] In "Philip
Massinger," Eliot distinguishes "artistic conscience" from
"theatrical skill."

> *The unnatural Combat,* in spite of the deft handling of
> suspense and the quick shift from climax to a new suspense,
> the first part of the play is the hatred of Malefort for his

---

[68] "The Music of Poetry," *loc. cit.,* p. 26.

[69] *Ibid.,* p. 25.

[70] "A Dialogue on Dramatic Poetry," *SE,* p. 45.

[71] *The Use of Poetry and the Use of Criticism,* pp. 45–47. Eliot quotes
Butcher's interpretation of the unities (p. 47) and concludes that if what
Butcher says is true, then "it should be obvious that the observance of
this Unity [i.e., emotional unity] must lead us, given certain dramatic mate-
rial otherwise highly valuable, inevitably to violation of the Unities of
Place and Time."

son and the second part is his passion for his daughter. It
is theatrical skill, not an artistic conscience arranging emotions, that holds the two parts together.[72]

Massinger, Eliot proceeds to say, "as an artisan of the theater
. . . is not inferior to Fletcher, and his best tragedies have an
honester unity than *Bonduca*. But the unity is superficial."
The "synthetic cunning" of Massinger's "theatrical skill"
"welds" but not "unifies."[73] He is a "master of technique"
but no "artist." In contrast to Massinger, Jonson is a true
artist; he unifies rather than welds.

> Jonson employs immense dramatic constructive skill: it is
> not so much skill in plot as skill in doing without a plot.
> He never manipulates as complicated a plot as that of *The
> Merchant of Venice*; he has in his best plays nothing like
> the intrigue of Restoration comedy. In *Bartholomew Fair*
> it is hardly a plot at all; the marvel of the play is the be-
> wildering rapid chaotic action of the fair; it is the fair
> itself, not anything that happens to take place in the fair.
> In *Volpone*, or *The Alchemist*, or *The Silent Woman*, the
> plot is enough to keep the players in motion; it is rather
> an "action" than a plot. The plot does not hold the play
> together; what holds the play together is a unity of inspira-
> tion that radiates into plot and personages alike.[74]

Poetic technique consists in "a recognition of the truth
that not our feelings but the pattern which we make of our
feelings is the center of value."[75] Poetic form is accountable
to the type of emotional order (or disorder) a poet chooses
to deal with. Massinger is "eloquent of emotional disorder";
Shakespeare, in his plays, analyzes one emotion after another
into its constituents; and Dante's *Commedia* deals with the

---

[72] "Philip Massinger," *SE*, p. 187.

[73] *Ibid.*

[74] "Ben Jonson," *SW*, p. 115.

[75] "A Brief Introduction to the Method of Paul Valéry," *loc. cit.*, p. 12.

most comprehensive order of human emotions. Such differences in emotional pattern dictate the structural differences between Massinger's romantic comedies, Shakespeare's
tragedies, and Dante's vast allegory.[76]

No less a problem of "emotional unity" is the problem of
dramatic characterization. "A character, to be living," says
Eliot, "must be conceived from some emotional unity. A
character is not to be composed of scattered observations of
human nature, but of parts which are felt together."[77] Conflicts among characters (or within a character) reflect the
human soul's struggles toward emotional order, "moral synthesis," and self-organization. It is from such moral struggles and resolutions that dramatic plot draws its unity and
dramatic characters derive their reality.

> It is in fact in moments of moral and spiritual struggle
> depending upon spiritual sanctions . . . that men and wom-
> en come nearest to being real.

> Some dramatists can effect a satisfying unity and signifi-
> cance of pattern in single plays, a unity springing from
> the depth and coherence of a number of emotions and feel-
> ings, and not only from dramatic and poetic skill. The
> *Maid's Tragedy*, or *A King and No King*, is better con-
> structed, and has many poetic lines, as *The Changeling*, but
> is far inferior in the degree of inner necessity in the feel-
> ing. . . .[78]

Plot construction and characterization thus are contingent
upon the "continuous moral formulations" of the soul. Ulti-

---

[76] "Dante," *SW*, p. 168: "Shakespeare takes a character apparently controlled by a simple emotion, and analyses the character and emotion itself.
The emotion is split up into its constituents—and perhaps destroyed in
the process. . . . Dante . . . does not analyse the emotion so much as he
exhibits its relation to other emotions."

[77] "Philip Massinger," *loc. cit.*, p. 188.

[78] *After Strange Gods*, p. 45, and *SE*, p. 171. Cf. *supra*, p. 13, n. 24.

mately, poetic unity must be sought in the unity of the soul. Simply because of the lack of order in the soul, plays such as *Hamlet* and poets such as Massinger become formless.

Eliot was delighted to see Jonson define "imitation" as the ability "to convert the substances, or riches of another poet, to his own use."[79] The distinction between true and false imitation for Eliot is essentially a distinction between unificaton and combination, assimilation and aggregation.

> Immature poets imitate; mature poets steal; bad poets deface what they take, and good poets make it into something better, or at least something different. The good poet welds his theft into a whole of feeling which is unique, utterly different from that from which it was torn; the bad poet throws it into something which has no cohesion.[80]

The "good poet," in other words, has a "point of view," a "soul," which imposes a "form" on reality and in which everything is given a new place and a new significance. What is artistically relevant is not the source of the materials but their successful integration. And artistic unity is to be sought, ultimately, in "the whole of feeling which is unique," the "world" which is a "point of view."

RESOLUTION

When the principle of analysis is shifted from Coherence and Correspondence to Comprehensiveness, poetry is viewed by Eliot as an art of resolution rather than as one of transmutation and organization. The quality of wit completes, together with unity and intensity, the trinity by which poetry may be identified and evaluated. Wit, according to Eliot, is supposed to be found whenever opposites are re-

---

[79] *The Use of Poetry and the Use of Criticism*, p. 55.

[80] "Philip Massinger," *loc. cit.*, p. 182.

solved and similarity in dissimilars is perceived. Figurative use of words in all its varieties (stichomythia, pun, conceit, metaphor) is said to contain one element or another of wit. In a pun, one word is given two applications, or two different words are held together by one sound. And in a conceit "far-fetched comparison" is made and concealed similarity ("hidden relation") is disclosed. "In a conceit," remarks Eliot, "two things very different are brought together, and the spark of ecstacy generated in us is perception of the power in bringing them together. The intellectual pleasure in this ingenuity is what we call wit."[81] And in "Mystic and Politician as Poet," Eliot finds "pure wit" in the "rapid and bewilderingly clever succession of conceits."[82] Wit, however, is not supposed to be a mere verbal technique. For paradox of ideas, irony in dramatic situation, and sophistry of emotion equally involve wit.

> Take a poem like "The Prohibition." It is neatly constructed. The first stanza is a development of its first line, "Take heed of loving me." The second develops the opposite thought, "Take heed of hating me." The third combines the two, "Yet, love and hate me too." The whole is a good example of what Dryden and Johnson call "wit": it develops two ideas and unites them in a paradox.[83]

Cyrano's speech on the nose, we are told, exhibits a species of wit which arises from dramatic irony whereas Donne's "The Prohibition" shows a wit of ideas. Wit of situation occurs when a dramatic character begins to see himself as others would see him. "For when any one is conscious of himself as acting, something like a sense of humour is pres-

---

[81] "Andrew Marvell," *Nation and Athenaeum*, XXXIII (1923), 809.

[82] "Mystic and Politician as Poet: Vaughan, Traherne, Marvell," *Listener*, III (1930), 591.

[83] "Rhyme and Reason: The Poetry of John Donne," *loc. cit.*, p. 502.

ent."[84] "The really fine rhetoric of Shakespeare occurs," remarks Eliot, "in situations where a character in the play *sees himself* in a dramatic light";[85] and wit is found in "the self-consciousness and self-dramatization of the Shakespearean heroes," in "the attitude of self-dramatization assumed by ... heroes at moments of tragic intensity," and in the adoption by a character of an "aesthetic" attitude in his "dramatizing himself against environment."[86] The pride and resignation of the dying heroes in Shakespeare is neither comic nor tragic but something beyond each and comprehensive of both—an "alliance of levity and seriousness."[87] Sophistication in situation and in emotion is also found in Jonson. In *Catiline*, the scene between Fluvia and Gulla and Sempronia "is no more comedy than it is tragedy."[88] And the Prologue of Sylla's ghost is highly self-conscious.[89] "We can see," remarks Eliot, "for Shakespeare or Jonson, that each had in the end a personal point of view which can be called neither comic nor tragic."[90] Their "point of view," in Eliot's terminology, is "sophisticated"; and wit is a "sophisticated" virtue.

Sophistication of emotion in Shakespeare's songs, Eliot

---

[84] "Rhetoric and Poetic Drama," *SE*, p. 29.

[85] *Ibid.*, p. 27.

[86] "Shakespeare and the Stoicism of Seneca," *SE*, pp. 110 ff.

[87] "Shakespearean Criticism: From Dryden to Coleridge," *A Companion to Shakespeare Studies*, ed. Harley Granville-Barker and G. B. Harrison (Cambridge, 1934), p. 295: "For to those who have experienced the full horror of life, tragedy is still inadequate. Sophocles felt more of it than he could express, when he wrote *Oedipus the King;* Shakespeare, when he wrote *Hamlet;* and Shakespeare had the advantage of being able to employ his grave diggers. In the end, horror and laughter may be one—only when horror and laughter have become as horrible and laughable as they can be;—whatever the conscious intention of the authors—you may laugh or shudder over *Oedipus* or *Hamlet* or *King Lear*—or both at once: then only do you perceive that the aim of the comic and tragic dramatist is the same: they are equally serious." See also "Thomas Middleton," *loc. cit.*, p. 141.

[88] *SE*, p. 131.   [89] *Ibid.*, pp. 129–30.   [90] *Ibid.*, p. 141.

holds, is achieved through a mutual intensification of the emotion of the form and the emotion of the subject. In Shakespeare's songs, says Eliot, "the form, the pattern of movement, has a solemnity of its own, however light and gay the human emotion concerned; gaiety of its own however serious and tragic the emotion."[91] Marvell's *To His Coy Mistress* also shows a wit of similar kind. "There lies a tough reasonableness beneath the slight lyrical grace," "an alliance of levity and seriousness"[92]—"a divine levity" and "holy mirth," which Johnson's *London*, for instance, lacks.[93] Wit, thus, is not an "occasional embellishment" but a "spirit animating the whole composition."[94] (The wit of Dryden consists in the magnification of the trivial as the wit of Pope in the diminution of the great.)[95]

The concept of wit as an art contingent upon the resolution of the opposites has a technical as well as a more elevated application. The mutual intensification of opposing emotions and the resolution of conflicting thoughts may well be construed as technical matters. But on the other hand, the removal of contradictions implies the perception of unity in diversity which constitutes the solid basis of Wisdom, Charity, and Light. Eliot concedes that Johnson's treatment of wit as a rhetorical device is a useful one. But he considers Cowley's definition of wit in the *Ode of Wit* the more profound—for Cowley realizes that wit is a mode of activity basic to the universal process of unification and characteristic of the divine order.

---

[91] "Introduction," *Selected Poems by Marianne Moore*, p. xiv.

[92] "Andrew Marvell," *SE*, pp. 252, 255.

[93] "A Note on Two Odes of Cowley," *Seventeenth Century Studies Presented to Sir Herbert Grierson* (Oxford, 1938), p. 242.

[94] *Ibid.*, p. 239.

[95] "John Dryden," *loc. cit.*, pp. 266–67, 269.

In a true piece of Wit all things must be
   Yet all things there agree;
As in the Ark, joined without force or strife,
All creatures dwelt, all creatures that had life.

Or as the primitive forms of all
(If we compare great things with small)
Which, without discord or confusion, lie
In that strange mirror of the Deity.[96]

Wit becomes "noticeable by itself" only in the abuse or misuse of the technique of wit that appears in the minor poets. The abuses of wit are faulty conceits, irrelevant puns, and distended metaphors and similes; they never consist in sentimentality nor false sublimity. In its higher manifestations wit becomes "imagination" (as Coleridge once defined it), and merges into "the religious comprehension of life"— λόγος ζυνός —"the fullest understanding of life."[97]

The wise man, in contrast to the merely worldly-wise on the one hand, and the man of some intense vision of the heights or the depth on the other, is one whose wisdom springs from spiritual sources, who has profited by experience to arrive at understanding and who has acquired the charity that comes from understanding of human beings in all their variety of temperament, character and circumstances.[98]

Eliot compares wit to erudition, for both imply "richness in experience." He separates wit from erudition, for erudition does not necessarily involve reconciliation and unification, which is basic to wit. Eliot compares wit to cynicism, for cynicism, like wit, implies a "constant inspection of ex-

---

[96] "A Note on Two Odes of Cowley," *loc. cit.*, pp. 235–36. These lines were first quoted in "Andrew Marvell," *loc. cit.*, p. 261.

[97] "Andrew Marvell," *loc. cit.*, p. 256; "Goethe as the Sage," *loc. cit.*, p. 264.

[98] "Goethe as the Sage," *loc. cit.*, p. 258.

periences." But to Eliot cynicism is not wit, for cynicism involves the negation of all, whereas wit demands the assimilation of each.[99] The "poise," "balance," and "equilibrium" achieved in ironies and paradoxes through the coincidence of contraries reflects, however faintly and remotely, the "serenity" of soul life, the "sanity" of vision, the "centrality" of viewpoint, and the "urbanity" of "wise" man.[100] "Wisdom is communicated on a deeper level than that of logical propositions; all language is inadequate, but probably the language of poetry is the language most capable of communicating wisdom."[101] To Eliot, poetry is the "language of wisdom" and "wisdom is an essential element in making poetry."[102]

Variations in Eliot's critical concepts and terms, doctrines and tenets, distinctions and analogies, as we may see now, are all derived from the prismatic activity of his dialectic of Unity. As principles of Comprehensiveness, Coherence, and Correspondence are proposed by turns, dichotomies used to frame critical discussions shift from pair to pair, and definitions of art and poetry multiply. When Correspondence is made the basis of analysis, art is considered as an art of expression (for meaning must be arrested in form), and poetry is spoken of as equivalence and symbol. When Coherence is considered, art is treated as an art of composition (for details must be organized into form), and poetry is spoken of as design and music. And when Comprehensiveness is

---

[99] "Andrew Marvell," *SE*, p. 262.

[100] *Ibid.*, p. 263: "The quality which Marvell had, this modest and certainly impersonal virtue—whether we call it wit or reason, or even urbanity—we have patently failed to define. By whatever name we call it, and however we define that name, it is something precious and needed and apparently extinct."

[101] "Goethe as the Sage," *loc. cit.*, p. 258.

[102] *Ibid.*

appealed to, art is treated as an art of communication (for truth can be stated only in the form of tropes and paradoxes), and poetry is spoken of as wit and wisdom.

The "fluidity" of Eliot's critical concepts, however, is not only conditioned by the shifting of basic dichotomies; it is also made possible by the expansion and restriction of the meaning of the same set of opposites. Form, design, and wit have each a "religious" as well as a "technical" application. Wit, in its lower applications, refers to the "rhetorical" figures. But in its higher applications, it is conceived as the direct manifestation of Divine wisdom and related to such lofty Christian ideas as Love, Charity, and Light (which Eliot once expounded in "Virgil and the Christian World").[103] The higher and lower meanings of wit, however, are kept in harmony all the time through the concept of wit as an awareness of the same in the other.

With equal "fluidity" he employs the terms form and design. Design, in its technical applications, concerns itself with the disposition of words, images, and episodes; but artistic order, in its higher applications, is conceived as an approximation of the ecumenical vision where the many is resolved into one. The poet is the conductor to Reality as he is an eductor of Truth:

> For it is ultimately the function of art, in imposing a credible order upon ordinary reality, and thereby eliciting some perception of order *in* reality, to bring us to a condition of serenity, stillness, and reconciliation; and then leave us, as Virgil left Dante, to proceed toward a region where that guide can avail no farther.[104]

And, finally, symbol, in its lower applications, is a matter related to the supply of form to matter, medium to content.

---

[103] "Virgil and the Christian World," *PP*, pp. 147–48. Love, for instance, was conceived there as "a principle of order in the human soul."

[104] "Poetry and Drama," *PP*, p. 94.

But in its elevated applications, it involves the perception and realization of the spirit in nature. Art is separable from morals and religion when the meaning of art is restricted to the construction of "sensuous equivalence." But once problems concerning the nature of reality and appearance are raised, art can no longer be isolated from religion, for perfect art consists in perfect perception, which is spiritual perception:

> . . . esthetic sensibility must be extended into spiritual perception, and spiritual perception must be extended into esthetic sensibility and disciplined taste before we are qualified to pass judgment upon decadence or diabolism or nihilism in art. To judge a work of art by artistic or by religious standards, to judge a religion by religious or artistic standards should come in the end to the same thing: though it is an end at which no individual can arrive.[105]

The triad of Comprehensiveness, Coherence, and Correspondence are distinctive moments of Unity, yet they are closely allied. For the resolution of opposites means the perception of a higher reality and more inclusive order just as the unification of parts involves the perception of sameness in difference and significance in appearance. Thus, terms like wit, form, and symbolism all have a threefold definition. Symbolism means not only the "incarnation of meaning in fact," but also the creation of a "pattern" of meanings—"to find the word and give it the utmost meaning, in its place; to mean as many things as possible, to make it both exact and comprehensive, and really to unite the disparate and remote, to give them a fusion and a pattern within the word."[106] Form refers to the perception of significance as well as to the order such perception may bring about. In "Ulysses,

---

[105] *Notes towards the Definition of Culture*, p. 29.

[106] "Preface," *Transit of Venus*, p. viii.

Order and Myth," Eliot identifies the artistic method with
the mythical method, which is supposed to reduce chaos
into order, confusion into significance.[107] "A myth," he defines, "is a point of view raised to importance by imagination."[108] Eliot offers, in "A Note on Two Odes of Cowley,"
to define wit three ways. He defines it in the context of
Comprehensiveness as "holy mirth," which involves the resolution of such opposed attitudes as the tragic and the comic.
He defines it in the context of Correspondence as a "balance" of the emotional with the intellectual value. And he
defines it in the context of Coherence as "the exceptional
power of creating a unity of feeling out of the most disparate elements." "In the loosest of Donne's compositions,"
Eliot observes, "there is a kind of continuity in change, and
we can perceive an effect of wit throughout the whole
which is not merely the sum of the wit of the parts."[109] I
name the three moments of Unity as Correspondence, Coherence, and Comprehensiveness for two reasons: (1) the
alliterative effect suggests unity in variety, and (2) Eliot indicates in his doctoral dissertation that these three are the
basic conditions of "experience," or "finite center,"[110] which
poetry prefigures.

---

[107] "Ulysses, Order and Myth," *Dial,* LXXV (1923), 480–83.

[108] "Notes on Current Letters," *Tyro,* I (1922), 4.

[109] "A Note on Two Odes of Cowley," *loc. cit.,* pp. 239, 242.

[110] See chap. v, pp. 117 ff., "Configuration."

The Nature of Classicism

PERSONALITY

The dialectic of Unity not only operates in Eliot's formulation of the conditions of art, it is also active in his conception of the requirements of the poet. Eliot's discussion of the poet concentrates upon two major problems: his internal cohesion and his external concord. The poet may be viewed as a composite whole exhibiting a pattern of interests and attitudes, which is his personality. On the other hand, he may be viewed as a component part participating in the activities of such larger wholes as tradition and culture; in his function as a participant, he is supposed to conform to and cohere with other poets, and, indeed, ultimately with other human beings—as men are individuals in communion with God. "A poet," says Eliot, "like a scientist, is contributing toward the organic development of culture."[1] The dialectic seeks its way into Eliot's formulation about the poet through the intermediaries of such familiar doctrines as actualization (of potentialities), organization (of interests), and maturation (through resolution of opposing elements). And both the problems of internal cohesion and external concord can be reduced to problems describable in terms of

---

[1] "Contemporanea," *Egoist*, V, No. 6 (1918), 84.

unity in diversity, identity in difference, and continuity in change.

Never for a moment does Eliot lose sight of the larger frame of reference of the unity of human beings in the Kingdom of God, yet his immediate critical concern is the internal coherence of the poet. "The whole of Shakespeare's works," Eliot points out, "is *one* poem, and it is the poetry of it in this sense, not the poetry of isolated lines and passages or the poetry of the single figures which he created, that matters most."[2] "A man," he continues, "may, hypothetically, compose a number of fine passages or even whole poems which would each give satisfaction, and yet not be a great poet, unless we felt them to be united by one significant, consistent and developing personality."[3]

> The standard set by Shakespeare is that of a continuous development from first to last, a development in which the choice both of the theme and of dramatic and verse technique in each play seems to be determined increasingly by Shakespeare's state of feeling, by the particular stage of his emotional maturity at the time. What is "the whole man" is not simply his greatest or maturest achievement, but the whole pattern formed by the sequence of plays; so that we may say confidently that the full meaning of any one of his plays is not in itself alone, but in that play in the order in which it was written, in its relation to all of Shakespeare's other plays, earlier and later: we must know all of Shakespeare's works in order to know any of it. No other dramatist of the time approaches anywhere near to this perfection of pattern, of pattern superficial and profound; but the measure in which dramatists and poets approximate to this unity in a lifetime's work is one of the measures of major poetry and drama.[4]

The presence of a unified personality behind a poet's works suggests the basis for Eliot's distinction of the "ma-

---

[2] *SE*, p. 179.   [3] *Ibid.*   [4] *Ibid.*, pp. 170–71.

jor" poet from the "minor." Whereas the minor poet pro-
duces what Eliot speaks of as "anthology pieces," each of
which is unrelated to another, the works of a major poet are
marked by "a unity of underlying pattern," which is the
poet's "particular comprehension of life," his "point of
view," and his "personality." The distinction between the
major and minor poet enables Eliot to treat poetic works not
merely as discrete wholes but as constituent parts which are
fully intelligible only in the larger organization of the poet's
selfhood. As pattern may be simple or complex, as order
may be restricted or inclusive, the scale of poetic achievement can consequently be infinitely elaborated and flexibly
treated. Not only is Shakespeare distinguishable from such
chaotic souls as Ford, Massinger, Beaumont, Fletcher, Shir-
ley, and Otway; he is also separable from Marlowe, Jonson,
Chapman, Middleton, Webster, and Tourneur, all of whom
show a measure of unity. "The nearest to him," remarks
Eliot, "is Marlowe. Jonson and Chapman have the consistency, but a far lower degree of significant development;
Middleton and Webster take a lower place than these; the
author of *The Revenger's Tragedy*, whether we call him
Tourneur or Middleton or another, accomplishes all that
can be accomplished within the limits of a single play."[5] On
a still higher level of comparison, Shakespeare himself appears restricted in his point of view, for the organization of
his soul is evidently of an order inferior to Dante's.[6]

Since higher poetry consists in the synthetic activity of
the soul in the formation of a selfhood, it is essential for the
poet of the better kind to effect a personal integration of
materials available to him and to forge a personal form of
expression. The poor poet pours his "liquid sentiment into a

---

[5] *Ibid.*, p. 179.   [6] *SW*, p. x.

ready-made mould.'"[7] Or, he remains formless as Massinger
did.

> Marlowe's and Jonson's comedies were a view of life; they
> were, as great literature always is, the transformation of
> a personality into a personal work of art, their lifetime's
> work, long or short. Massinger is not simply a smaller
> personality; his personality hardly exists. He did not, out
> of his own personality, build a world of art, as Shakespeare
> and Marlowe and Jonson built.[8]

Eliot's "Critical Note" prefaced to the *Collected Poems of
Harold Monro* maintains that the poet must express "the
spirit of one man" and must pursue "personal idiom" and
"personal vision."[9] Eliot praised Harry Crosby, for Crosby
had engaged himself in the search of "personal symbolism of
imagery" and a personal apprehension of life.

> Crosby was right, very right, in looking for a set of sym-
> bols which should relate each of his poems to the others,
> to himself, rather than using in each poem symbols which
> should merely relate it to other poems by other people. . . .
> Harry Crosby's verse was consistently, I think, the result
> of an effort to record as exactly as possible to his own
> satisfaction a particular way of apprehending life.[10]

A "genuine" poet is an "individualist" in the sense that his
productive activities are activities of self-integration and
self-organization. Ready conformity to stock expressions,
stock feelings, and stock ideas betrays the absence of that
synthetic energy basic to the formation of a unique self.
Poets, therefore, may be spurious and inferior simply because they exhibit a sensibility which is "ordinary" and "impersonal." "The sensibility of Heywood," says Eliot, "is

---

[7] *PP*, p. 30.   [8] *SW*, p. 139.

[9] "A Critical Note," *loc. cit.*, p. xv.

[10] "Preface," *Transit of Venus*, p. vii.

merely that of ordinary people in ordinary life."[11] "Ford's poetry, as well as Beaumont and Fletcher's," remarks Eliot, "is of the surface; that is to say, it is the result of the stock expressions of feeling accumulated by the greater men."[12] The Georgian poets Eliot describes as "impersonal," for their vision "belongs to the sensibility of the ordinary sensitive person, not primarily only to that of the sensitive poet; it is not always easy to distinguish the work of one author from the work of another."[13] Nor does Eliot spare Tennyson:

> It is important that the artist should be highly educated in his own art; but his education is one that is hindered rather than helped by the ordinary processes of society which constitute education for the ordinary man. For these processes consist largely in the acquisition of impersonal ideas which obscure what we really are and feel, what we really want, and what really excites our interest. It is of course not the actual information acquired, but the conformity which the accumulation of knowledge is apt to impose, that is harmful. Tennyson is a very fair example of a poet almost wholly encrusted with parasitic opinion, almost wholly merged into his environment.[14]

Collectivism in all its modern varieties, Eliot holds, is "hostile to art." For the domination of "herd feeling" and "mass consciousness" only hastens the coagulation of the "surface of existence" and speeds the destruction of the originality and sincerity which are basic to the poet.

> We are already accustomed to seeing, from time to time, immense numbers of men and women voting all together, without using their reason and without enquiry; so per-

---

[11] *SE*, p. 153.   [12] *Ibid.*, p. 180.

[13] "A Critical Note," *The Collected Poems of Harold Monro*, p. xiv.

[14] *SW*, p. 154.

haps we have no right to complain of the same masses singing all together, without much sense of tune or much knowledge of music; we may presently see them praying and shouting hallelujahs all together, without much theology or knowledge of what they are praying about. We cannot explain it. But it should at present be suspect; it is very likely hostile to art; and it may mark, and be a measure of hastening the disappearance of the English individualist whom we have heard so much about in the past, and his transformation into the microscopic cheese-mite of the great cheese of the future.[15]

The "impersonal" mode of perception is contrary to the nature and function of poetry: for poetry

may effect revolutions in sensibility such as are periodically needed; may help to break up the conventional modes of perception and valuation which are perpetually forming, and make people see the world afresh, or some new part of it. It may make us from time to time a little more aware of the deeper, unnamed feelings which form the substratum of our being, to which we rarely penetrate; for our lives are mostly a constant evasion of ourselves, and an evasion of the visible and sensible world.[16]

As a result of Eliot's conception of poetry as self-realization and self-integration, the characteristics of a given poet's personality, the reflection of such characteristics in his art, and the pattern of his artistic and personal development all become distinctive areas of analysis. It is with these problems in view that Eliot offers to discuss, for instance, the poetry of Byron, Yeats, and Kipling in "Byron" (1936), "Yeats," (1940), and "Kipling" (1948). To Eliot, Byron exemplifies the extreme of personal poetry and is conscious of his own selfhood even to the extent of making it a deliberate intel-

---

[15] "Commentary," *Criterion*, V (1927), 286.

[16] *The Use of Poetry and the Use of Criticism*, p. 155.

lectual construction—"he was an actor who devoted immense trouble to *becoming* a role that he adopted."[17] "It is only the self that he invented that he undertsood perfectly."[18] Byron, in Eliot's words, "fabricates" a self; and this fabricated self supplies the essential vitality to his art. Eliot treats Byron primarily as a "story-teller" who is master of the art of "divagation."

> The effect of Byron's digression is to keep us interested in the story-teller himself, and through this interest to interest us more in the story. On contemporary readers this interest must have been strong to the point of enchantment; for even still, once we submit ourselves to the point of reading a poem through, the attraction of the personality is powerful.[19]

Eliot recognizes a quality of "foreignness" in Byron: "Byron was not 'in *this* people,' either of London or of England, but in his mother's people."[20] This "foreignness" is clearly reflected both in Byron's language and vision. "Byron," says Eliot, "writes a dead or dying language";[21] "I cannot think of any other poet of his distinction who might so easily have been an accomplished foreigner writing English."[22] Byron's alien vision, moreover, creates his bitter sense of isolation, breeds his hatred of English hypocrisy, and nurses his posture of damnation.[23]

The development of Kipling's poetry, we are told, coincides with the change of his outward circumstances. His change in residence (from India to Sussex) brings about his change in poetic vision (from the imperialistic imagination to the historical imagination). The imperialistic imagination

---

[17] *PP*, p. 238.

[18] *Ibid.*, p. 235.

[19] *Ibid.*, p. 227.

[20] *Ibid.*, pp. 233–34.

[21] *Ibid.*, p. 232.

[22] *Ibid.*, p. 233.

[23] *Ibid.*, p. 238.

of Kipling's earlier years and the historical imagination of his
maturity, however, are both rooted in his idea of the Empire
as generated by his characteristic sensibility—a sensibility
keen to the affairs of the world about him rather than to his
own joys and sorrows, to his own feelings in their similarity
to those of other men rather than in their particularity.[24]
Kipling's personality, in the best sense of the word, is a
"commonplace" personality.[25] Consequently, the particular verse form that he excelled in is "balladry."[26] There is
variety and development in Kipling's works, yet the whole
displays a significant unity. "No part of Kipling's work,
and no period of his work, is wholly appreciable without
taking into account the others; and in the end, this work,
which studied piecemeal appears to have no unity beyond
the haphazard of external circumstances, comes to show a
unity of a very complicated kind."[27]

Eliot contrasts Yeats with Kipling. First, external events
do not account for Yeats's development. It is, we are made
to understand, "the integrity of his passion for his art and
his craft" that "provided such an impulse for his extraordi-
nary development."[28] Secondly, unlike Kipling, who has a
"commonplace" vision, Yeats elevates his private passions
into universal truth.[29] If Kipling is a balladist, then Yeats is a
lyric poet. (Lyric means "rather a certain kind of selection
of emotion than particular metrical form.")[30] Yeats, we are
told, is "a poet who in his work remained in the best sense
always young, who even in one sense became young as he
aged."[31] In Yeats, "the most lively and desirable emotions
of youth have been preserved to receive their full and due

---

[24] *Ibid.*, p. 285.   [27] *Ibid.*, p. 272.

[25] *Ibid.*   [28] *Ibid.*, p. 296.   [30] *Ibid.*, p. 303.

[26] *Ibid.*, p. 271.   [29] *Ibid.*, p. 299.   [31] *Ibid.*, p. 302.

expression in retrospect."[32] Yeats "had to wait for a later maturity to find expression of early experience; and this makes him, I think, a unique and especially interesting poet."[33]

For Eliot, so long as a poet's work evidences the synthetic operation of self-integration, it warrants his claim to be a "major" poet. Consequently, what is to be sought in the major poet is such characteristics as unity in variety, identity in difference, and continuity in change. And these features, Eliot observes, can be manifest in an œuvre of long poems, or in one single long poem having sufficient variety in unity, or in a collection of short poems which, "taken individually, may appear rather slight." *The Vanity of Human Wishes* and *The Deserted Village*, Eliot believes, have the "proper unity and variety" to assure the greatness of Johnson and Goldsmith. "I should myself regard Samuel Johnson as a major poet by the single testimony of *The Vanity of Human Wishes*, and Goldsmith by the testimony of *The Deserted Village*," declares Eliot.[34] Herrick is a major poet, we are told, because behind his short poems there is a unifying personality.[35] So is George Herbert.

> *The Temple* is, in fact, a structure, and one which may have been worked over and elaborated, perhaps at intervals of time, before it reached its final form. We cannot judge Herbert, or savour fully his genius and his art, by any selection to be found in an anthology; we must study *The Temple* as a whole.
>
> To understand Shakespeare we must acquaint ourselves with all of his plays; to understand Herbert we must acquaint ourselves with all of *The Temple*.[36]

---

32 *Ibid.*, p. 303; see also p. 299.   34 *Ibid.*, p. 44.

33 *Ibid.*, p. 299.   35 *Ibid.*, p. 43.

36 *George Herbert*, p. 15; cf. PP, p. 42.

"So in the end," says Eliot, "I, for one, cannot admit that Herbert can be called a 'minor' poet: for it is not of a few favorite poems that I am reminded when I think of him, but of the whole work."[37] "All I have affirmed is," he continues, "that a work which consists of a number of short poems, even of poems which, taken individually, may appear rather slight, may, if it has a unity of underlying pattern, be the equivalent of a first-rate long poem in establishing an author's claim to be a 'major' poet."[38]

TRADITION

In Eliot's criticism, the poet is conceived either as a composite whole of distinctive interests and attitudes, or as a component part participating in the synthetic operation of a larger whole. Tradition is one such larger frame of reference to which Eliot frequently refers the poet. The dialectic of Unity operates in the formulation of the concept of tradition through the intermediary of the doctrine of the "adjustment" between the "old" and the "new." For Eliot, tradition consists of sequences of resolution. Once a tradition is formed, it is immediately expected to move toward an order of more inclusive unity through the assimilation and participation of new parts. Characteristic of Eliot's dialectic, such a synthetic process is conceived as a double operation involving the readjustment of the old order for the accommodation of the new as much as the cohesion of the new with the established order.

> The necessity that he [the poet] shall conform, that he shall *cohere*, is not one-sided; what happens when a new work of art is created is something that happens simultaneously to all the works of art which precedes it. The

---

[37] *PP*, pp. 42–43.   [38] *Ibid.*, p. 44.

existing monuments form an ideal order among themselves, which is modified by the introduction of the new
(the really new) work of art among them. The existing
order is complete before the new work arrives; for order
to persist after the supervention of novelty, the *whole*
existing order must be, if ever so slightly, altered; and so
the relations, proportions, values of each work of art toward the whole are readjusted; and this is the conformity
between the old and the new.[39]

The conception of tradition as a dynamic whole yields a
number of negative definitions. Tradition, in the first place,
is not supposed to be a "lump"; nor is it a repetition; nor is it
an evolution. For an "indiscriminate bolus" is a whole without definite parts; repetition furnishes no new parts; and
evolution involves the replacement of the old by the new.[40]
For Eliot, continuity and change are both basic to tradition.
As change assures the diversity of parts so continuity secures
the identity of the whole. In Eliot's discussion of the poet,
the distinction between originality and eccentricity is important. For eccentricity (or oddity) is a quality of the *disjecta membra*, whereas originality belongs to those parts
that are constituent members of a whole and yet retain their
own individuality.[41] Tradition is exposed to the danger of
"petrifaction" when order becomes static and incapable of
assimilation. It is threatened with "dissolution" if the new
parts are odd and eccentric. "Preservation" keeps the identity of the continuum which is tradition, whereas "experi-
mentation" brings to it freedom of expression. Tradition ad-
mits experiment, yet it is a movement of "destiny."

---

[39] *SW*, pp. 49–50.

[40] *Ibid.*, pp. 48, 51.

[41] "A Brief Introduction to the Method of Paul Valéry," *loc. cit.*, p. 4;
cf. "Introduction," *Ezra Pound: Selected Poems* (London, 1928), pp. x–xi.

By tradition, I do not mean its vainglories, its conceit of itself in its past; but the fact it has grown in one way and not in another, and that its future growth is determined in certain directions, if any, by its having grown in that way through the past.[42]

Eliot's conception of tradition provides room for originality, but originality as he conceives it is a consequence of the individuation of the One.

"We cannot be primarily interested in any writer's nerves . . . or in any one's heredity except for the purpose of knowing to what extent that writer's individuality distorts or detracts from the objective truth which he perceives. If the writer sees truly—as far as he sees at all—then his heredity and nerves do not matter.[43]

Nowhere else than in his interpretation of the doctrine of imitation has Eliot so fully disclosed his treatment of tradition as a process of self-affirmation through self-completion. One knows one's self only when one knows one's own place in the whole scheme of things.

Poets arrive at originality by different routes. Some, by progressive imitation; though the word imitation is truly applicable only to the successes of the negligible; for those who have something in them, the process is rather towards a finding of themselves by a progressive absorption in, and absorption of, and rejection (but never a total rejection) of other writers.[44]

The "historical sense" is an instrument of self-discovery, for it is an instrument for the discovery of the whole. When the whole pattern of artistic activity is perceived, the past and the present fall into proper places, their significances are

---

[42] "Commentary," *Criterion*, XIV (1934), 88.

[43] "Poet and Saint . . . ," *Dial*, LXXXII (1927), 427.

[44] "Preface," *Transit of Venus*, p. v; cf. "Introduction," *Selected Poems by Ezra Pound*, p. x.

revealed, and what is permanent in them may be separated from what is accidental.

> The historical sense involves a perception, not only of the pastness of the past, but of its presence; the historical sense compels a man to write not merely with his own generation in his bones, but with a feeling that the whole of the literature of his own country has a simultaneous existence and composes a simultaneous order. This historical sense, which is a sense of the timeless as well as of the temporal and of the timeless and the temporal together, is what makes a writer traditional. And it is at the same time what makes a writer most acutely conscious of his place in time, of his own contemporaneity.[45]

Tradition, in its ultimate designation, consists in the timeless order that comprehends all the necessary parts and from which each part derives its significance. Seán Lucy was right when he observed that Eliot "has a vision of a sort of 'City of God' in literature."[46] For Eliot, the republic of letters in its final arrangement is, like the City of God, an orderly whole.

> We suppose not merely a corpus of writings in one language, but writings and writers between whom there is a tradition; and writers who are not merely connected by tradition in time, but also are related so as to be in the light of eternity contemporaneous, from a certain point of view cells in one body, Chaucer and Hardy. We suppose a mind which is not only the English mind of one period with its prejudices of politics and fashions of taste, but which is a greater, finer, more positive, more comprehensive mind than the mind of any period. And we suppose to each writer an importance which is not only individual, but due to his place as a consistent part of this mind.[47]

---

[45] *SW*, p. 49.   [46] Lucy, *op. cit.*, p. 14.
[47] "Was There a Scottish Literature?" *Athenaeum*, No. 4657 (1919), p. 680.

The historical sense brings "maturity" to the mind in that it involves perception of the whole and integration of the parts. With a slight adjustment of the concept, the historical sense may be applied to such synthetic activity of the mind as is involved at the critical juncture of cultural integration. The "classic," Eliot holds, is a product of the "maturity of mind"; but

> maturity of mind: this needs history, and the consciousness of history. Consciousness of history cannot be fully awake, except where there is another history than the history of the poet's own people: we need this in order to see our own place in history. There must be the knowledge of the history of at least one other highly civilized people, and of a people whose civilization is sufficiently cognate to have influenced and entered into our own.[48]

Eliot considers the *Aeneid* a "classic" on the ground that it shows the reconciliation of two great civilizations "under an all-embracing destiny."

> It is this development of one literature, or one civilization, in relation to another, which gives a peculiar significance to the subject of Virgil's epic. In Homer, the conflict between the Greeks and the Trojans is hardly larger in scope than a feud between one Greek city-state and a coalition of other states; behind the story of Aeneas is the consciousness of a more radical distinction, a distinction which is at the same time a statement of *relatedness*, between two great cultures, and, finally, of their reconciliation under an all-embracing destiny.[49]

ORTHODOXY

Eliot seeks the perfection of poetry in the perfection of Unity. Unlike Aristotle, who treats poetic works as given wholes and looks for causal explanation of their specific fea-

---

48 *PP*, p. 62.   49 *Ibid.*, pp. 62 ff.

tures in terms of the matter, manner, form, and purpose involved, Eliot identifies Unity as the essence of poetry and
resolves to determine poetic hierarchy on the basis of the
degrees of Unity manifest in works and poets. Consequently, the study of poetry for Eliot is the study of sequences of
unification and levels of synthesis, with the perfection of
total experience and the state of the Kingdom of God as its
ultimate frame of reference. It is, indeed, no accident that
Eliot's concern with the ideal of Christian society, the state
of the Holy Roman Empire, and the unity of Europe should
be manifested time and again in his critical writings.[50] For
Eliot's inquiries into the conditions of the perpetuation and
refinement of values, the organization and development of
"common culture," and the maintenance and renewal of
"orthodoxy," all have direct bearings upon the study of
poetry. And the final construction of the poetic hierarchy
must fall back upon careful discrimination of the degrees in
which poetry participates in the universal operation of synthesis and approximates the perfect state of divine wisdom.

As Correspondence, Coherence, and Comprehensiveness
are all but aspects of Unity, the perfection of poetry may be
expressed in various ways as the perfection of the truth and
value it expresses, the excellence of the order it brings about,
and the breadth of its scope of resolution. In the dialectic of
Eliot, the formation of "common" value is treated as a matter of organic "growth," involving both the conscious formulations and unconscious feelings of a social community.
Characteristically, Eliot, in *After Strange Gods*, bifurcates
the "social sanction" of value into two parts: "tradition" and

---

[50] See, for instance, "[A Letter to the Editor, F. M. Ford]," *Transatlantic Review*, Vol. I (1924); "Commentary," *Criterion*, Vol. VI, No. 2 (1927); *Die Einheit der Europäischen Kultur* (Berlin, 1946); "Preface," *The Dark Side of the Moon* (New York, 1947), p. x.

"orthodoxy." Here Eliot readjusts the term "tradition," equates it with communal habits and communal feelings, and contrasts it with "orthodoxy," which is supposed to be the formulated system of common beliefs—"a matter which calls for the exercise of all our conscious intelligence."[51] Tradition, says Eliot,

> is rather a way of feeling and action which characterizes a group throughout generations; and . . . it must largely be, or . . . many of the elements in it must be, unconscious.[52]

And again,

> What I mean by tradition involves all those habitual actions, habits and customs, from the most significant religious rite to our conventional way of greeting a stranger, which represents the blood kinship of "the same people living in the same place."[53]

It is through the mutual adjustment of communal intellect and communal sensibility (tradition and orthodoxy), that common ethos is secured and common vision is achieved: "Tradition by itself," Eliot observes, "is not enough; it must be perpetually criticised and brought up to date under the supervision of what I call othodoxy."[54] "The habits of the community" must be constantly "formulated, corrected, and elevated by the continuous thought and direction of the Church."[55]

The method of maintaining the "orthodoxy of sensibility" Eliot outlines with even greater clarity in *The Idea of a Christian Society*, where he contends that the perpetuation of value requires the interplay between the Christian community (which practices) and what he chooses to call the

---

[51] *After Strange Gods*, p. 19.

[52] *Ibid.*, p. 29.   [54] *Ibid.*, p. 62.

[53] *Ibid.*, p. 18.   [55] *Ibid.*, p. 54.

Community of Christians (which formulates).[56] Thought-
ful schemes and abstract theories might be unreal unless they
are proved to be "livable" communally and sanctioned by
constant practices. On the other hand, behaviors and cus-
toms would become meaningless unless they are periodically
raised to a state of high consciousness. It is through the
mutual qualification between the conscious formulations of
the Community of Christians (the "clerisy") and the unconscious feelings of the Christian community (the "con-
gregation") that values are perpetuated and refined. And, in
such a process of development and growth, the Community
of Christians may even admit "disbelievers" into their com-
pany, if the "disbelievers" prove to be of "exceptional intelligence."[57]

At the top of Eliot's poetic hierarchy there is what he
calls the "classics." A classic, according to Eliot, expresses
the "common vision" in a "common style," which is the
synthesis of the "whole range of feelings of a people" and
which is achievable only through the collective effort of a
race. Thus in "Blake," Eliot distinguishes "genius" from the
"classic," and, with the following passage, he concludes his
study of the "naked man" Blake.

> Blake has been endowed with a capacity for considerable
> understanding of human nature, with a remarkable and
> original sense of language and the music of language, and
> a gift of hallucinated vision. . . . What his genius required,
> and what it sadly lacked, was a framework of accepted
> and traditional ideas which would have prevented him
> from indulging in a philosophy of his own. . . . The con-
> centration resulting from a framework of mythology and
> theology and philosophy is one of the reasons why Dante
> is a classic, and Blake is only a man of genius.[58]

---

[56] *The Idea of a Christian Society*, p. 34.
[57] *Ibid.*, p. 35.   [58] *SW*, p. 157.

A classic, then, is the expression of the ethos of a culture rather than the intensity of a private vision. And, all other things being equal, the superiority of a classic is in proportion to the completeness of the system of value that it expresses. Strictly speaking there are only two "classics" in the whole of European literature, Dante and Virgil. Virgil speaks for Latin civilization in its maturity and Dante gives expression to Christian culture in its high point. Of the two European classics, Dante, Eliot holds, is undoubtedly the superior one. For although Virgil adequately presents such values as labor, piety and destiny, the higher ideal of Unity as embodied in such concepts as Light, Love, and Charity did not find its full expression until the arrival of Dante.[59] In its comprehensiveness, the empire of Virgil is one grade lower than the world of Dante. Eliot does not choose to erect Dante as the poetic model to be imitated directly by modern poets, for the complication of experience in modern life calls, once more, for new synthesis and therefore new expression. Yet he recognizes that no new classic will emerge unless a new ecumenical vision is established and the Holy Roman Empire is restored to its proper order. Pellegrini's interview recorded Eliot's profound veneration for Dante. "Then," wrote Pellegrini,

> we came to talk of Dante, as the poet in whom ecumenical unity and faith are expressed; Eliot alluded to his veneration for Dante, and concluded to us, today, having not been vouchsafed the attainment of that inner coherence between faith and poetry: we can only admire its supreme exemplar in the greatest poet who ever lived.[60]

The classics may be divided, through a simple dichotomy, into the Christian and pre-Christian; or they may be di-

---

[59] *PP*, pp. 142, 144, 147, 148.

[60] Alessandro Pellegrini, "A London Conversation with T. S. Eliot," *Sewanee Review*, LVII (1949), 291.

vided, in a similar manner, into the local and universal. For the purpose of opposing the universal classics against the local ones, Eliot makes Dante join hands with Virgil. For, in Eliot's opinion Virgil, like Dante, is "European" in contrast with such a "provincial" poet as Pope, who presents only a local synthesis of values in an age which witnessed "the disintegration of Christendom."

> In the eighteenth century, we are oppressed by the limited range of sensibility, and especially in the scale of religious feeling. . . . And this restriction of religious sensibility itself produces a kind of provinciality: . . . the provinciality which indicates the disintegration of Christendom, the decay of common belief and common culture.[61]

As social mechanism grows out of the demands of valuable activities, so culture is a social creation. Society and culture both rely upon religion for purpose and meaning—without religion society and culture will die out of "boredom."[62] On the other hand, religion requires society and culture to embody and refine the system of values which it adumbrates—only in the "primitive" society does the simple religious-social-artistic complex of a ritual exist.[63] Society, thus, is a "spiritual community" rather than the aggregation of a mob; and culture is "the incarnation (so to speak), of religion" rather than a flurry of uncoordinated activities.[64] The interdependence of religion, culture, and society Eliot clearly outlines in his sociological studies, *The Idea of a Christian Society* and *Notes towards the Definition of Culture*. For him, to assert that common culture and ordered society are essential conditions for the production of classics is the

---

[61] *PP*, p. 61; cf. "Disjecta Membra," *Egoist*, V (1918), 55: "Provinciality of point of view is a vice."

[62] *SE*, p. 316. Also cf. *Notes towards the Definition of Culture*, p. 32.

[63] *Notes towards the Definition of Culture*, pp. 29–30, 67.

[64] *Ibid.*, p. 27.

same as to assert that classics depend upon the vitality of religion. The alternation of the classic and romantic ages Eliot therefore equates to the alternation of the theistic and secular ages. By a single cause, he tries to account for the conditions of poetry in modern times. The history of Europe since the Great Schism, says he, can be written as the rise of romanticism in literature, the dissolution of society, and the decay of the Faith.[65]

> The chief clue to the understanding of most contemporary Anglo-Saxon literature is to be found in the decay of Protestantism. . . . It is this background, I believe, that makes much of our writing seem provincial and crude in the major intellectual centers of Europe—everywhere except Northern Germany and perhaps Scandinavia; it is this which contributes the prevailing flavour of immaturity.[66]

The contrast between unity and chaos, from which Eliot draws his differentia of theism from secularism, receives a more specific treatment in *After Strange Gods* as a contrast between the centrality of orthodoxy and the eccentricity of personality.

> When morals cease to be a matter of tradition and orthodoxy—that is, of the habits of the community formulated, corrected, and elevated by the continuous thought and direction of the Church—and when each man is to elaborate his own, the PERSONALITY becomes a thing of alarming importance.[67]

The chaos of the modern world, Eliot points out, arises from the romantic taste for the "different":

> What is disastrous is that the writer should deliberately give reign to his "individuality," that he should even cultivate his differences from others; and that his readers

---

[65] *Ibid.*   [66] *After Strange Gods*, p. 41.   [67] *Ibid.*, p. 54.

should cherish the author of genius, not in spite of his deviations from the inherited wisdom of the race, but because of them.[68]

In *After Strange Gods* Eliot repeats the Platonic assault upon the poet as a false prophet in adoration of strange gods of one kind or another. His criticism of Yeats and Lawrence is quite representative.

> Mr. Yeats' "supernatural world" was the wrong supernatural world. It was not a world of spiritual significance, not a world of real Good and Evil, of holiness and sin, but a highly sophisticated lower mythology summoned, like a physician, to supply the fading pulse of poetry with some transient stimulant so that the dying patient may utter his last words.[69]

As for Lawrence:

> The point is that Lawrence started life wholly free from any restriction of tradition or institution, that he had no guidance except the Inner Light, the most untrustworthy and deceitful guide that ever offered itself to wandering humanity.[70]

In its diagnosis of the illness of the modern world, in its attack upon romanticism, Professor Babbitt's humanism has the appearance of "orthodoxy."[71] But humanism of Bab-

---

[68] *Ibid.*, p. 35. The classicist is, of course, interested as much in the sameness as in the difference, see "Commentary," *Criterion*, XI (1932), 678: "And anyone who is committed to religious dogma must also be committed to a theory of art which insists upon the permanent as well as the changing, which cares as much, let us say, about the resemblances between the draughtsmanship of Hokusai and Pollaiho as it does about the difference."

[69] *After Strange Gods*, p. 50.   [70] *Ibid.*, p. 64.

[71] "Revelation," *Revelation*, ed. John Baillie and Hugh Martin (New York, 1937), pp. 15–16: "What makes him [Babbitt] unique is that, while himself a disbeliever, even an opponent of revealed religion, he attacked the foundations of secularism more deeply and more comprehensively than any other writer of our time. His mind, on its periphery, touching questions and philosophies of our time, might be the mind of a Christian; and except from a Christian standard, I do not see how we can object to his conclusions."

bitt's variety relies too much upon "the intellectual and individual effort."[72] It offers little emotional consolation and
excites no enthusiasm because it ignores the role of communal wisdom which orthodoxy and tradition generate. His
philosophy, therefore, Eliot observes, encourages "heresies"
and is itself a product of the romantic age, reflecting the
"heretical" spirit.

Ants Oras is right in asserting that Eliot's critical system
was "a kind of extremely subtle National Economy, in
which everybody found some useful part."[73] The "National
Economy," however, is not generated from some preconceived utilitarian scheme as Oras seems to imply; it springs
rather from a dialectical necessity derived from the assumption of the essential indivisibility of activities and the ultimate unity of experience. Seen from a broader point of view,
diversity is a condition of unity and what at first appears to
be "eccentric" may turn out finally to be part of the synthetic operation that prevails in the universe. "In many instances," writes Eliot, "it is possible that an indulgence of
eccentricities is the condition of the man's saying anything
at all."[74]

Wordsworth, Shelley, and Goethe, Eliot indicates, "belong with the numbers of the great heretics of all times."
"It is," however,

> not a wilful paradox to assert that the greatness of each of
> these writers is indissolubly attached to his practice of the
> error, of his own specific variation of the error. Their
> place in history, their importance for their own and sub-
> sequent generations, is involved in it; this is not a purely
> personal matter. They would not have been as great as

---

[72] *After Strange Gods*, p. 43.

[73] Ants Oras, *The Critical Ideas of T. S. Eliot* (Tartu, 1932), p. 68.

[74] *After Strange Gods*, p. 32.

they were but for the limitations which prevented them from being greater than they were.[75]

"Furthermore," says Eliot,

> the essential of any important heresy is not simply that it is wrong: it is that it is partly right. It is characteristic of the more interesting heretics, in the context in which I use the term, that they have an exceptionally acute perception, or profound insight, of some part of the truth; an insight more important often than the inference of those who are aware of more but less acutely aware of anything. So far as we are able to redress the balance, effect the compensation, ourselves, we may find such authors of the greatest value.[76]

"Classicism," concludes Eliot, "is not an alternative to 'romanticism.' . . . It is a goal toward which all good literature strives, so far as it is good, according to the possibilities of its place and time."[77] "One can be classical in tendency by doing the best one can with the material at hand."[78]

Recognizing diversity as a condition of the ever-expanding Unity, Eliot proposes the progress of history to be "cyclical." "Maturity" of mind is preceded and followed by eccentricities. And since the quality of language reflects the quality of sensibility, the "cycle" is also evident in the alternate sequence of "eccentric" and "common" style.

> The age which precedes a classic age, may exhibit both eccentricity and monotony: monotony because the sources of the language have not yet been explored, and eccentricity because there is yet no generally accepted standard —if, indeed, that can be called eccentric where there is no

---

[75] *The Use of Poetry and the Use of Criticism*, pp. 99–100.

[76] *After Strange Gods*, p. 24.

[77] "Ulysses, Order, and Myth," *James Joyce*, ed. Seon Givens (New York, 1948), p. 200.

[78] *Ibid.*

center. Its writing may be at the same time pedantic and licentious. The age following a classic age, may also exhibit eccentricity and monotony: monotony because the resources of the language have, for the time at least, been exhausted, and eccentricity because originality comes to be more valued than correctness. But the age in which we find a common style, will be an age when society has achieved a moment of order and stability, of equilibrium and harmony; as the age which manifests the greatest extremes of individual style will be an age of immaturity or an age of senility.[79]

"The proper end of the romantic," Eliot affirms, "is to achieve the classic—that is to say, every language, to retain its vitality, must perpetually depart and return upon itself; but without the departure there is no return, and the returning is as important as the arrival."[80]

---

[79] *PP*, p. 57.

[80] "Leçon de Valéry," *Paul Valéry* (Marseille, 1946), p. 78.

The Problems of Criticism

TASTE AS A PROCESS OF ORGANIZATION

I thought of literature then, as I think of it now [observes Eliot], of the literature of the world, of the literature of Europe, of the literature of a single country, not as a collection of the writings of individuals, but as "organic wholes," as systems in relation to which, individual works of literary art and the works of individual artists, have their significance.[1]

The concept of world poetry as an organic whole demands, from criticism, a twofold task: criticism should not only examine and evaluate a work of art in the light of the laws of its own perfection, it should also place a work of art in the total context of literature so that its particular defect or excess might be discerned. The critic is not only to "analyze" but also to "compare." He is engaged in the elucidation of art and the artist as well as in the "correction of taste." This double operation of the critic may be exemplified by Eliot's own criticism of Milton. The Hertz Lecture

---

[1] "The Function of Criticism," *SE*, pp. 12–13. Also see *SW*, p. 49: "No poet, no artist of any sort, has his complete meaning alone. His significance, his appreciation is the appreciation of his relation to the dead poets and artists. You cannot value him alone; you must set him, for contrast and comparison, among the dead." Cf. "Mr. Lucas's Webster," *Criterion*, VII (1928), 156.

tries to elucidate the beauties of Milton in terms of his "magniloquence," whereas the essays of *Homage to John Dryden* attempt to show "magniloquence" as a consequence of the "dissociation of sensibility" and the excess of the "auditory imagination," thereby condemning it as a perversion of language and sensibility.[2] On the ground that Charles Whibley has failed to employ the standards of the whole for the judgment of the parts, Eliot condemns him as an "imperfect critic."

> He has not the austerity of passion which can detect unerringly the transition from work of eternal intensity to work that is merely beautiful, and from work that is beautiful to work that is merely charming. For the critic needs to be able not only to saturate himself in the spirit and fashion of a time—the local flavour—but also to separate himself suddenly from it in an appreciation of the highest creative work.[3]

Eliot thus broadly distinguishes criticism into two kinds, the romantic and the classical. Romantic criticism claims that "the law of art is all case law,"[4] whereas classical criticism, upholding the "classical ideal," strives to approximate the absolute standard which may be derived from the whole of poetry.

For Eliot, if a critic is to accomplish his appointed tasks satisfactorily, he must seek to reconstruct for himself an order of world literature. And the development of taste consists in the approximation to the "organic whole," which is the poetry of the world. The one inevitable problem the

---

[2] "The Metaphysical Poets," *loc. cit.*, p. 247; "Andrew Marvell," *loc. cit.*, p. 260; "John Dryden," *loc. cit.*, p. 268; "Milton I," *loc. cit.*, pp. 159, 162; "Milton II," *PP*, p. 176.

[3] "Imperfect Critics," *SW*, p. 37.

[4] "The Function of Criticism," *loc. cit.*, pp. 17–18.

critic has finally to face is how to perfect the organization of his own aesthetic experiences. Characteristically for Eliot, it is in terms of the organization of experience that he describes the nature of criticism. Critical propensity, we are told, is natural to man and present in the ordinary reader— "A large number of people, I believe, have the native capacity of enjoying some *good* poetry." The critic, however, is engaged in the organization and reorganization of his own aesthetic experiences for the purpose of arriving at an ultimate order. Thus, in *The Use of Poetry and the Use of Criticism*, Eliot discriminates three steps in the development of taste—enjoyment, appreciation, and criticism.

> A large number of people, I believe, have the native capacity of enjoying some *good* poetry. It is only the exceptional reader, certainly, who in the course of time comes to classify and to compare his experiences, to see one in the light of others; who, as his poetic experiences multiply, will be able to understand each more accurately. The element of enjoyment is enlarged into appreciation, which brings a more intellectual addition to the original intensity of feeling. It is a second stage in our understanding of poetry, when we no longer merely select and reject, but organize. We may even speak of a third stage, one of reorganization; a stage at which a person already educated in poetry meets with something new in his own time, and finds a new pattern of poetry arranging itself in consequence.[5]

Once more the dialectic of Unity finds its way into Eliot's thought. His formulation of the nature of criticism is essentially a formulation of the adjustment of parts, the resolution of conflicts, and the constant movement toward an ever more inclusive "pattern" and "order."

---

[5] *The Use of Poetry and the Use of Criticism*, pp. 18–19.

What taste is, I suppose, is an organization of immediate
experiences obtained in literature, which is individually
modified in its shape by points of concentration of our
strongest feelings, the authors who have affected us most
strongly and deeply. It cannot be had without effort,
and without it, our likings remain insignificant accidents.
To be immediately and without effort pleased by Donne
is easy for some people, to be in the same way moved by
Shelley is easy for another; the difficulty lies in that
process which is not of abstract thought, but which is
an organization of feeling, making possible, not only to
appreciate Shelley in one mood and Donne in another,
but the inclusion of even greater diversity into a system
of perception and feeling.[6]

The critic's "view" is continuously modified by increasing
experience, and he has "to take stock of the situation afresh"
at every stage of his development.[7] The critic, however, sits
in judgment not only of art and the artist but also in judgment of all other critics. And different tastes must themselves finally fall into a "pattern" and "order."

One of the errors, I think, of critical theory, is to con-
ceive one hypothetical poet on the one hand, and one
hypothetical reader on the other. It is perhaps a less dangerous error than to have no hypothesis at all. My point
is that the legitimate motives of the poet, and also the
legitimate responses of the reader vary very widely, but
that there is a possible order in the variations.[8]

Viewed in the broader scheme of things, variations in
criticism are complementary. Two factors contribute to
determine the difference of individual taste: the "personal-

---

[6] "The Education of Taste," *Athenaeum*, No. 4652 (1919), p. 521.

[7] "Poetry and Drama," *loc. cit.*, p. 75.

[8] "Poetry and Propaganda," *Literary Opinions in America*, ed. M. D.
Zabel (New York, 1951), p. 103.

ity" of the critic and the "group personality" of his time. Apart from individual modification of taste resulting from the pull and push of personality, there is the social modification, for prepossessions of an age often draw critical attention to one aspect or another of poetry. For instance, "in the works of Shakespeare critics of the past, we can see, when we have made the deduction of individual genius and individual limitations, the outlines of the consciousness of the critic's age."[9] When Eliot joins the form-matter dichotomy with his division of the ordered and chaotic society, there appears his dialectical construction of the transitions in English criticism. The change from criticism of form to criticism of content, according to Eliot, closely corresponds to the transition of the English society from a relatively stable moral and religious order to moral confusion and religious dissolution.

Eliot inverted Arnold's distinction between the critical age and the creative age. What would have been a critical age to Arnold appears to be creative to Eliot (creative of value); and what would have been a creative age appears to him critical (critical of form). Campion, Sidney, Ben Jonson, and Dryden, Eliot holds, were all technical critics who lived in a relatively stable society. Their attention was mainly directed to such problems as rhyme in verse, unities in drama, and invention, disposition, and elocution in composition. Gradually technical interests diminished; and, with the steady decline of religious faith and the poet's eventual assumption of the prophetic role, critics began to take serious interest in the possibility of poetry serving as a substitute for religion and philosophy. They directly involved themselves

---

[9] "Introduction," *Shakespeare and the Popular Dramatic Tradition*, p. 7.

in the general search for a new outlook on life, a new cultural order, and a new value system.

Signs of transition, Eliot contends, were found in Addison, but with Addison poetry continued to delight and entertain. Johnson's technical predilections isolated him from his own age and kept him in the back eddy of history rather than in the main stream. Critics in the nineteenth century were characteristically attracted to poetry as social expression (Wordsworth), to the philosophical depth of poetic vision (Coleridge), and to the kinetic mission of the poet (Shelley). In the hands of Arnold, the poet was inaugurated as the critic of life and the custodian of culture; Pater presented his doctrine of life for art's sake under the thinly disguised pretext of art for art's sake. In more recent times, the sociological analysis of poetic mission (Belgion) and the psychological defense of poetry as the prime agency for a well-organized psyche (Richards) were new versions of the old argument that poetry is a substitute for ethics and religion.

If critical taste is subject to the pressure of social demands, it is no less free from the influence of personality.

> For the development of genuine taste, founded on genuine feeling, is inextricable from the development of personality and character. Genuine taste is always imperfect taste—but we are all, as a matter of fact, imperfect people; and the man whose taste in poetry does not bear the stamp of his particular personality, so that there are differences in what he likes from what we like, as well as resemblances, and differences in the way of liking the same things is apt to be a very uninteresting person with whom to discuss poetry.[10]

---

[10] *The Use of Poetry and the Use of Criticism*, pp. 35-36.

"We have to see literature through our own temperament in order to see it at all,"[11] declares Eliot. And, a "personal point of view" Eliot holds as basic to the critic.[12]

> Each act of appreciation is a progress toward maturity: the very different views of life, cohabiting in our minds, affect each other, and our own personality asserts itself and gives each a place in some arrangement peculiar to our self.[13]

"Although," he continues, "there is an objective ideal of orthodox taste in poetry, no one reader can be, or should try to be, quite orthodox."[14] "The objective ideal of orthodox taste" consists in the "pattern" of critical points of view that history discloses; and only in the perspective of time can limitations of individual taste be shown.

> Each age demands different things from poetry, though its demands are modified, from time to time, by what some new poet has given. So our criticism, from age to age, will reflect the things that the age demands; and the criticism of no one man and of no one age can be expected to embrace the whole nature of poetry or exhaust all of its uses. Our contemporary critics, like their predecessors, are making particular responses to particular situations. No two readers, perhaps, will go to poetry with quite the same demands. Amongst all these demands from poetry and responses to it there is always some permanent element in common, just as there are standards of good and bad writing independent of what any one of us happens to like and dislike; but every effort to formu-

---

11 "Experiment in Criticism," *The Bookman*, LXX (1929), 225.

12 In "Criticism in England," *Athenaeum*, No. 4650 (1919), p. 457, Eliot listed "sensitiveness, intelligence, curiosity, intensity of passion, infinite knowledge, and a personal point of view" as the requirements of a critic.

13 "Poetry and Propaganda," *loc. cit.*, p. 106.

14 "What Is Minor Poetry?" *PP*, p. 46.

late the common element is limited by the limitations of particular men in particular places and at particular times; and these limitations become manifest in the perspective of history.[15]

Eliot believes there are absolute critical standards, yet in his appoach to these standards, he adopts some relativistic devices.

> We must assume, if we are to talk about poetry at all, that there is some absolute poetic hierarchy; we keep at the back of our minds the reminder of some end of the world, some final Judgment Day, on which the poets will be assembled in their ranks and orders. In the long run, there is an ultimate greater or less. But at any particular time, and we exist only in particular moments of time, good taste consists, not in the attaining to the vision of Judgment Day, and still less in assuming that what happens to be important for us now is certainly what will be important in the same way on that occasion, but in approximating to some analysis of the absolute and the relative in our own appreciation.[16]

In the works of Eliot, individual taste is by turns defended and condemned, as a permanent standard is proposed yet withdrawn.[17] It is evident that Eliot's conception of criticism is part of the broader scheme of his dialectic of the permanent and the transitory. Critics, like poets and moralists, aspire to the conditions of eternal truth, yet whatever truth they possess is limited by here and now. In the following credos he combines his "profound skepticism" with his "profound faith."

---

[15] *The Use of Poetry and the Use of Criticism*, pp. 141–42.

[16] "Donne in Our Time," *loc. cit.*, p. 5.

[17] Eliot's condemnation of the interference of "temperament" in criticism is recurrent; see *SW*, esp. p. 40.

It seems to me, accordingly, that the humane and civilized faith must comprehend all the others. We must believe, first, that the human race can, if it will, improve indefinitely; that it can improve both its material well-being and its spiritual capacities. We must also have a conception of a perfect society attainable on earth. And we must also admit the inadequacy of these ambitions and ideals. We must say that man, however he is improved by social, economic reorganization, by eugenics, and by any other external means possible to the science of intellect, will still be only the natural man, at an infinite remove from perfection. And we must affirm that perfection is as nearly attainable for man here and now as it ever will be in any future in any place. That there can be no art greater than the art which has already been created: there will only be different and necessarily different combinations of the eternal and changing in the forms of art. That men individually can never attain anything higher than has been already attained among the saints; but that in any place, at any time, another saint may be born. Such a just perception of the permanent relations of the Enduring and the Changing should on the one hand make us realize our own time in better proportion to times past and times to come. . . . And on the other hand it should help us to think better of our time, as not isolated and unique, and remind us that fundamentally our individual problems and duties are the same as they have been for others at any time—and equally our opportunities.[18]

MODES OF CRITICISM

The nature of criticism may be analyzed in terms of the organization of experiences, or it may be stated in terms of the transmutation of impressions. In Eliot's formulation of criticism, the principle of Correspondence is as active as the

---

[18] "A Commentary," *Criterion*, XII (1932), 78.

principle of Coherence. With little difficulty the dichotomy
of one and many may be replaced by the dichotomy of
thought and feeling. For the organization of experiences of
art implies the erection of "laws of good taste"—"ériger en
lois ses impressions personnelles, c'est le grand effort d'un
homme s'il est sincère."[19] The growth of the structure of
artistic experiences also means the refinement of critical
principles. And, criticism, it may be said, consists in the
"quiet coöperative work" of intellect and sensibility.

> But I believe that it is always opportune to call attention
> to the torpid superstition that appreciation is one thing,
> and "intellectual" criticism something else. Appreciation
> in popular psychology is one faculty, and criticism an-
> other, an arid cleverness building theoretical scaffolds
> upon one's own perceptions or those of others. On the
> contrary, the true generalization is not something super-
> imposed upon an accumulation of perception; the
> perceptions do not, in a really appreciative mind, ac-
> cumulate as a mass, but form themselves as a structure;
> and criticism is the statement in language of this structure;
> it is the development of sensibility.[20]

With a slight adjustment of terms, Eliot, in "The Frontiers
of Criticism," made "understanding" and "sympathy" the
two limits of critical activity. Contemporary criticism,
either in the form of the "lemon-squeezer" criticism of
Empson or the "hermeneutics" practiced by Livingstone
Lowes, is mainly a product of understanding, and, therefore, only partially satisfies the conditions of criticism.

The stages involved in the transmutation of artistic experience suggest two basic modes of criticism, the artistic and
the philosophical. Criticism is not independent of but a part
of the creative efforts. For the poet is necessarily "critical"

---

[19] "The Perfect Critic," *SW*, p. 1.

[20] *Ibid.*, p. 15.

in his task of composition and construction—"the labor of shifting, combining, constructing, expunging, correcting, testing: this frightful toil is as much critical as creative."[21] And, "the critical mind operating *in* poetry, the critical effort which goes to the writing of it, may always be in advance of the critical mind operating *upon* poetry."[22] The artist's formulation of his own experience of creation reduces into precise "facts" what an ordinary reader can only vaguely feel.

> To the members of the Browning Study Circle, the discussion of poets about poetry may be arid, technical, and limited. It is merely that the practitioners have clarified and reduced to a state of fact all the feelings that the member can only enjoy in the most nebulous form; the dry technique implies, for those who have mastered it, all that the member thrills to; only that has been made into something precise, tractable, under control.[23]

Thus Eliot repeatedly asserts that "the workman's notes on the work form the most precious type of criticism."[24]

Perversions of artistic criticism occur either through excessive response or false generalization. Whereas good artistic criticism involves the transmutation of sensibility into understanding, impressionistic criticism "alters" rather than "transforms" the object of criticism. Critics like Walter Pater, or his disciple Arthur Symons, take the experience of art as a point of departure for the release of their own poetic emotion. Their criticism, Eliot remarks, is "etiolated creation."[25]

---

21 "The Function of Criticism," *loc. cit.*, p. 18.

22 *The Use of Poetry and the Use of Criticism*, p. 30.

23 "The Function of Criticism," *loc. cit.*, p. 20.

24 "Studies in Contemporary Criticism II," *Egoist*, V (1918), 132.

25 "A Brief Treatise on the Criticism of Poetry," *Chapbook*, II (1920), 2.

> The disturbance in Mr. Symons is almost, but not quite,
> to the point of creating; the reading sometimes fecun-
> dates his emotions to produce something new which is
> not criticism, but is not the expulsion, the ejection, the
> birth of creativeness. . . . Some writers are essentially
> of the type that reacts in excess of the stimulus, making
> something new out of the impressions, but suffer from
> a defect of vitality or an obscure obstruction which pre-
> vents nature from taking its course. Their sensibility
> alters the object, but never transforms it.[26]

Artistic criticism may degenerate into "impressionistic"
criticism through excessive response; or it may become
"dogmatic" criticism through false generalization. For "no
poet, when he writes of his own *art poétique*, should hope
to do much more than explain, rationalize, defend or pre-
pare the way for his own practice. That is, for writing his
own kind of poetry."[27] The poet-critic's theory is "a defence
of his conscious precepts of workmanship."[28] His aim, in
other words, is "limited," his primary concern being "to ex-
pound some novelty or impart some lesson to practitioners
of an art."[29] When the artist-critic (such as Horace or
Boileau) "pretends to erect a theory good for all time upon
his perception of what is needed for the present," when he
starts to "legislate" what is true to particular works as something universal and absolute, he is bound to be "dogmatic."[30]
   In contrast to artistic criticism Eliot proposes philosophical criticism, which concerns itself with the nature of poetry

---

[26] "The Perfect Critic," *SW*, p. 6.

[27] *From Poe to Valéry*, p. 16. Cf. "Mr. Murry's Shakespeare," *Criterion*, XV (1936), 708.

[28] *John Dryden: The Poet, the Dramatist, the Critic*, pp. 22–23.

[29] "The Perfect Critic," *SW*, pp. 11–12.

[30] *Ibid.*; "Preface," *English Poetry and Its Contribution to the Knowl-edge of a Creative Principle* (London, 1950), p. viii.

and aims at the production of absolute laws. Aristotle is a
"perfect" (philosophical) critic, for in his *Poetics* one finds
"intelligence itself swiftly operating the analysis of sensation
to the point of principle and definition."[31] Convinced of
the possibility of "common principle" and "outer authority,"
Eliot repudiates Spingarn's "creative criticism," which treats
criticism and poetry alike as "self-expression."[32] But Eliot
warns that philosophical criticism is "dangerous" to practice
and "the only excuse for it is unusual intelligence."[33] The
perversion of philosophical criticism comes from the substi-
tution of inquiring intelligence by emotional or verbal "generality."

> Whenever there is to be consideration of any group or
> number of writers, several activities may come into exist-
> ence: there are the feelings, emotions, direct impressions
> excited by immediate contact with the writer; there are
> the feelings, emotions, impressions aroused by contact
> and comparison of several writers, and there are the
> theories we may erect to account for these data. Also,
> there is the generality, which is usually a substitute for
> both impression and theory. . . . To communicate im-
> pressions is difficult; to communicate a co-ordinated sys-
> tem of impression is more difficult; to theorize demands
> vast ingenuity, and to avoid theorizing requires vast
> honesty. But to enunciate a generality is easy, and seldom
> useful.[34]

Technical criticism deals with particular objects, philosophical criticism with abstract laws. A third mode of criticism, however, may be suggested which intervenes between

---

[31] "The Perfect Critic," *SW*, pp. 11–12.

[32] "Creative Criticism," *Times Literary Supplement*, No. 1280 (1926),
535.

[33] "Studies in Contemporary Criticism II," *loc. cit.*, p. 132.

[34] "The Education of Taste," *loc. cit.*, p. 520.

108 Problems of Criticism

the particular and the absolute. With the aid of the perspective of time, the historical critic sets out to locate the common in the different, the permanent in the changing, so as to resuscitate the "living" element in the past and to bring the past to bear upon the solution of present problems. "To bring the poet back to life" is "the great, the perennial task of criticism."[35] And, "the important critic is the person who is absorbed in the present problems of art, and who wishes to bring the forces of the past to bear upon the solution of these problems."[36] The discovery of exemplars and the selection of touchstones, therefore, are among the most important functions of historical criticism.[37]

The perspective of history not only discloses the "meaning" of the past so that past exemplars can be summoned for the benefit of contemporary practitioners; in placing the present into the total context of artistic activities, it reveals also the limitations of the present. Only when equipped with the historical sense may the critic profitably embark upon his task of "correction of the taste" and serve as a "monitor of taste." The historical sense requires "erudition," and erudition "enables us to see literature all around, to detach it from ourselves, to reach a state of pure contemplation."[38] "The good critic," says Eliot, "is the man who, to a keen and abiding sensibility, joins wide and increasingly discriminating reading."[39]

---

[35] "Andrew Marvell," loc. cit., p. 251.

[36] "Imperfect Critics," loc. cit., pp. 37–38.

[37] J. C. Ransom, "The Historic Critic," T. S. Eliot: A Selected Critique, ed. L. Unger (New York, 1948), p. 57: "Eliot might be said to be a practitioner of Arnold's touchstone method of judging poetry, though with infinite refinement. . . ." "A historic critic . . . is a man with touchstones and a man who quotes."

[38] "Imperfect Critics," loc. cit., p. 40.

[39] "Religion and Literature," loc. cit., pp. 621–22.

> Those whose knowledge of poetry in the English language extends no further than to the immediate precursors of the poetry of our time, such as Hopkins and Yeats, or whose knowledge of the past is limited to the poetry extolled by some persuasive critic of the day (like myself), are limited in their understanding of the poetry that they do know. If, as I believe, poetry plays an important part in the process of education, then these readers are uneducated.[40]

The lack of historical sense yields two modes of critical perversion. Without historical insight, erudition may be reduced to scholarship. On the other hand, if history is not viewed as an evolution of the permanent in the changing but as mere flux, historical criticism may degenerate into historical relativism.

> Our preference for the changing over the permanent [says Eliot] manifests itself in various details of life. One instance is a prevalent tendency in literary criticism: the tendency to treat each work of art, especially those contemporary with ourselves, as a manifestation of the spirit of an age. The first-rate artist, the original writer, we say, is he who has most fully voiced this spirit; and when he has done this, he has done enough and has done well; our criticism consists in explaining what the spirit of the age is and how it is expressed in the writer's work.[41]

And again, "One of the consequences, as it seems to me, of our failure to grasp the proper relation of the Eternal and the Transient, is our over-estimation of the importance of our own time."[42] Historical criticism, for Eliot, is a mode of

---

[40] "On Teaching the Appreciation of Poetry," *Teachers College Record*, LXII (1960), 219–20.

[41] "Commentary," *Criterion*, XII (1932), 76.

[42] *Ibid.*, p. 75.

"wisdom" and a product of the "civilized" and "educated" mind. "By being 'educated,' " says Eliot,

> I mean having such an apprehension of the contours of the map of what has been written in the past, as to see instinctively where everything belongs, and approximately where anything new is likely to belong; it means, furthermore, being able to allow for all the books one has not read and the things one does not understand— it means some understanding of one's ignorance.[43]

Technical criticism, historical criticism, or philosophical criticism alone only partially fulfils the conditions of criticism. A complete criticism encompasses all these activities in their perfect excellence. And, "sensitiveness, erudition, sense of fact and sense of history, and generalizing power," are the basic qualifications of a "perfect critic."[44] The requirements for a complete Shakespearean critic that Eliot listed in his foreword to Henri Fluchère's *Shakespeare* provide a hint as to his awareness of the complexity and difficulty of criticism.

> The ideal Shakespeare critic should be a scholar, with knowledge not of Shakespeare in isolation, but of Shakespeare in relation to the Elizabethan Theatre in which he is only one, though very much the greatest of the masters, and of the Theatre in relation to the social, political, economic and religious conditions of its time. He should also be a poet; and he should be a "man of the theatre." And he should have a philosophic mind. Shakespeare criticism cannot be written by a committee consisting of a number of specialized scholars, a dramatist, a producer, an actor, a poet and a philosopher: each of them would be incompetent without sharing some of the knowledge and capacities of the other. Certainly,

---

[43] "Revelation," *loc. cit.*, p. 29.
[44] "The Perfect Critic," *loc. cit.*, p. 14.

to be a poet or a philosopher is not enough. A poet is not a qualified interpreter, unless he understands the particular technique of dramatic verse. In order to understand dramatic verse he must needs have had some success in writing it; and if his dramatic verse is to be really dramatic he must acquire also the point of view of the producer, the actor and the audience. To understand Shakespeare he must understand the theatre of his own time—and that of Shakespeare's time; he should know the latter, not merely as an antiquary, but from the point of view of the producer, the actor and the audience of Shakespeare's time. For such understanding, both scholarship and imagination are required. Nor is the philosophic critic, without the other qualification, in better case than the poet. The philosopher needs to understand the nature of poetry, if he is to avoid the danger of confusing the philosophical ideas which can be elicited upon a poem with a system of philosophical belief which can be attributed to the author. And it follows from what I have said above that he needs also to understand the special conditions of the stage, the peculiar kind of reality manifested by those personages of the stage who strike us as most "real," if he is to avoid the error of analysing dramatic characters as if they were living men and women, or figures from the historical past.[45]

Eliot himself has been engaged in the practice of all three modes of criticism. Assuming Unity as the essence of poetry, he seeks the best of poetry in the most refined and best balanced experience. Social community and cultural homogeneity thus are conceived as basic conditions for the production of "classics." Since culture and society depend upon religion for its unity, religion is ultimately considered as the basic condition of higher poetry. Better poets are not theo-

---

[45] "Foreword," *Shakespeare* by Henri Fluchère (London, 1953), pp. vi–vii.

logians and metaphysicians, yet they must have "orthodoxy of sensibility" and a "religious comprehension of life." The critical appreciation of poetry is an appreciation of the "civilized emotions" and "educated mind" as they are expressed in the language of wisdom. Superior poets can be distinguished from the inferior ones by their greater wisdom and civility. Better poets are "classical"; lesser poets are "romantic." And the difference between the "classical" and the "romantic" poets is "the difference between the complete and the fragmentary, the adult and the immature, the orderly and the chaotic."[46] With maturity of emotion and maturity of language as criteria, Eliot conducts his evaluation of poets and works.

The ultimate function of art, says Eliot, is "in imposing a credible order upon ordinary reality, and thereby eliciting some perception of order *in* reality, to bring us to a condition of serenity, stillness, and reconciliation."[47] The order that a work of art exhibits Eliot dichotomizes, in technical terms, into the verbal order and dramatic order—a poem presents "the two aspects of dramatic and of musical order." The technical analyses in "Poetry and Drama" emerge as analyses of human relationships evolving through a complex of incidents as well as analyses of stylistic devices of meter and diction. And the verbal equivalence and objective correlative are said to have derived their characteristics from the choice of the "theme," which is orthodox and symbolic in character—for the themes that *Murder in the Cathedral, The Family Reunion,* and *The Cocktail Party* deal with are drawn from "mythology." Thus in the analyses of his three verse plays, Eliot submits his "Poetry and Drama" as "practitioner's notes" and effects some technical formulations.

---

[46] "The Function of Criticism," *loc. cit.*, p. 15.

[47] "Poetry and Drama," *loc. cit.*, p. 94.

Finally, the exercise of the historical sense is evident, for instance, in Eliot's review of the Nonesuch edition of the *Love Poems of John Donne*. There the discussion falls into two parts: the diagnosis of contemporary taste and the elucidation of Donne's immediate relevance. The complexity and perplexity of the modern age are said to have reflected themselves in its false taste for Donne. Donne is being liked for the wrong reasons.

> In the poetry of Dante, or even of Cavalcanti, there is always the assumption of an ideal unity in experience, the faith in the ultimate rationalization and harmonization of experience, the subsumption of the lower under the higher, an ordering of the world more or less Aristotelian. But perhaps one reason why Donne has appealed so powerfully to the recent time is that there is in his poetry hardly any attempt at organization; rather a puzzled and humorous shuffling of the pieces; and we are inclined to read our own more conscious awareness of the apparent irrelevance and unrelatedness of things into the mind of Donne.[48]

And again,

> The age objects to the heroic and sublime, and it objects to the simplification and separation of the mental faculties. The objections are largely well grounded, and reacted against the nineteenth century; they are partly—how far I do not inquire—a product of the popularization of the study of mental phenomena. Ethics having been eclipsed by psychology, we accept the belief that any state of mind is extremely complex, and chiefly composed of odds and ends in constant flux manipulated by desire and fear. When, therefore, we find a poet who neither suppresses nor falsifies, who expresses a complicated state of mind, we give him welcome.[49]

[48] "John Donne," *Nation and Athenaeum*, XXXIII (1923), 332.
[49] *Ibid.*

But the real lesson Donne has to offer, Eliot suggests, is the unity in his complexity, order in chaos.

> The process which has carried us so far will carry us farther. The heroic and sublime, banished as reality, we take back as myth. . . . Neither the fantastic (Cleveland-ism is becoming popular) nor the cynical nor the sensuous occupies an excessive importance with Donne; the elements in his mind had an order and congruity. The range of his feeling was great, but no more remarkable than its unity.[50]

In showing Donne's contemporary relevance, Eliot achieves his historical criticism.

The critic attempts to supply technical analysis, evaluative standards, and historical perspective, but since all his analyses, standards, and perspectives depend upon the growth of the organization of his own experiences of art and of judgments on art, the best a critic can accomplish is to furnish "the conscious formula of a sensibility in the process of formation." Criticism impoverishes art, for any conscious formulation is by nature an abstraction, and as such must leave undiscussed certain aspects of the artistic object. In an interview with Iain Hamilton, Eliot refused to analyze his own dramatic personages.

> So far as I am concerned, I want to give the illusion of reality. . . . It seems to me that we should turn away from the Theatre of Ideas to the Theatre of Character. The essential poetic play should be made with human beings rather than with ideas. It is not for the dramatist to produce an analysed character, but for the audience to analyse the character. When the dramatist is creative, then the more creative the dramatist, the greater varieties of interpretation will be possible. There are more resources in the characters of Shakespeare than in most

---

[50] *Ibid.*

of the personages of modern prose drama, and the ways of interpreting them are endless. Drama is not poetic merely because it is in verse.[51]

But, on the other hand, criticism also enriches art,[52] for the critic brings into definite consciousness what the poet and the reader alike are unconscious of. Criticism furnishes grounds for "more intensified enjoyment through improved perception." And, the poet, like the reader, may benefit by critical formulations.

A new classical age will be reached when the dogma, or *ideology*, of the critic is so modified by contact with creative writing, and when the creative writers are so permeated by the new dogma, that a state of equilibrium is reached. For what is meant by a classical moment in literature is surely a moment of *stasis*, when the creative impulse finds a form which satisfies the best intellect of the time, a moment when a type is produced.[53]

---

[51] "Reflections on 'The Cocktail Party,'" *The World Review*, IX (1949), 22.

[52] The problem is stated in general terms in *Knowledge and Experience* (London, 1964), p. 22. Also see "The Music of Poetry," *PP*, p. 23.

[53] "Commentary," *Criterion*, II (1924), 232.

Conclusions:
Poetry as "Point of View"

CONFIGURATION

The multiple lines of investigation in Eliot's poetics converge in the concept of Unity. All Eliot's critical inquiries eventually revolve around the problems of transmutation, organization, and resolution, explainable in terms of the opposition and reconciliation of reality and ideality, unity and variety, and identity and difference. When the analysis moves from art through artist to society and steadily advances toward greater generality, what first appears as problems of symbols, structure, and wit (chap. ii) becomes problems of sincerity, integrity, and maturity, and of social order, cultural poise, and orthodoxy of sensibility. Consequently, the study of poetry for Eliot is the study of levels of synthesis and sequences of unification (chap. iii). Just as the poet needs the synthetic talent for the creation of poetry, the reader also requires that talent to respond fully to a work of art. The critic is supposed to be the most sensitive and intelligent of the audience, yet the critical mind itself is subject to the conditions of Unity. There is an ultimate poetic hierarchy, yet the individual critic (like the individual poet) proceeds only on perspective and experiment (chap. iv).

The whole of Eliot's criticism is a calculus of the conditions of unification. And the pattern of Unity set by the formation of experience is the central paradigm of poetry. It is in this connection that Eliot's doctoral dissertation, which (together with his two articles on Leibnitz) proposes a theory of experience, is relevant to this discussion.[1] Despite its many epistemological ramifications, Eliot's theory of experience is a fairly simple one. Eliot first assumes the existence of a whole of feeling out of which local consciousness arises through local concentration. In such local motion, combination and permutation of feeling take place. Through relationship, the "that" becomes a "what." The regulated relation of a cluster of feelings renders it a coherent whole and resolves its internal contradictions. And the articulation of the ideal content (the "whatness") of the feelings involved in the act of concentration makes it an act of expression. The act of concentration, which yields a complex of feeling which Eliot variously designates as experience, finite center, and point of view, is an act of transmutation, organization, and resolution. The configuration of feelings which is experience may be called the "finite center," for, although embedded in the whole of feeling, each configuration is a local concentration; it may be called "point of view," for, although prefigured in the vast unconsciousness, each configuration is a center of consciousness. "Higher soul life," says Eliot, consists in the "painful task of unifying (to a greater or less extent) jarring and incompatible worlds,

---

[1] "The Development of Leibnitz's Monadism," *Monist*, XXVI (1916), 534–56; "Leibnitz's Monads and Bradley's Finite Centers," *Monist*, XXVI, (1916), 566–76. These articles recently appeared as appendixes in Eliot's *Knowledge and Experience in the Philosophy of F. H. Bradley*, pp. 177–207.

and passing, when possible, from two or more discordant points to a higher which shall somehow include and transmute them."[2] The religious comprehension of life assumes the ultimate coherence of points of view, yet it turns out to be a point of view itself. "Bradley's universe," says Eliot, "actual only in finite centers, is only by an act of faith unified." So is Eliot's universe of points of view.

> Like monads, they [points of view] aim at being one; each expanded to completion, to the full reality latent within it, would be identical with the whole universe. But in so doing it would lose the actuality, the here and now, which is essential to the small reality which it actually achieves. The Absolute responds only to an imaginary demand of thought, and satisfies only an imaginary demand of feeling. Pretending to be something which makes finite centers cohere, it turns out to be merely the assertion that they do. And this assertion is only true so far as we here and now find it to be so.[3]

Eliot conceives the artistic process as a process of concentration, involving the configuration of feelings. It is in the language of configuration that Eliot describes, in the second section of "Tradition and the Individual Talent," the creative process. Genius, we are told, consists in the "more finely perfected medium in which special, or very varied, feelings are at liberty to enter into new combinations." "The poet's mind is in fact a receptacle for seizing and storing up numberless feelings, phrases, images, which remain there until all the particles which can unite to form a new compound are present together." "It is not the 'greatness,' the intensity, of the emotions, the components, but the intensity of the artistic process, the pressure, so

---

[2] *Knowledge and Experience*, p. 147.   [3] *Ibid.*, p. 202.

to speak, under which the fusion takes place, that counts."
"It is a concentration, and a new thing resulting from the
concentration, of a very great number of experiences which
to the practical and active person would not seem to be
experiences at all; it is a concentration which does not hap-
pen consciously or of deliberation."[4]

Poetry is "the precise statement of life which is at the
same time a point of view—a world which the author's mind
has subjected to a process of complete simplification."[5]
And, "in a man of scientific, or artistic temper, the personality is distilled in the work, it loses its accidents, it
becomes . . . a permanent point of view, in the history of
mind."[6] "I think that beauty of sound," says Eliot, "cannot be isolated, and the swift passage of thought does not
convey all the poet's intention; it is the swift communication of a vision or, rather, state of soul."[7] The great poet
is different from others exactly because he has a point of
view.

> Other men have had versatile talent, other men have
> restless curiosity, what characterizes the variety of in-
> terests and curiosity of men like Dante, Shakespeare and
> Goethe is the fundamental Unity. This unity is hard
> to define, except by saying that what each of them gives
> us is Life itself, the world seen from a particular point
> of view of a particular European age and a particular
> man of that age.[8]

----

4 "Tradition and the Individual Talent," *loc. cit.*, pp. 54, 55, 58. This
famous essay is evidently a revision and condensation of his extension
lecture which appeared later as "Modern Tendencies in Poetry," *Shama'a*, I
(1920), 9–18.

5 "The Possibility of Poetic Drama," *loc. cit.*, p. 68.

6 "Humanist, Artist, and Scientist," *Athenaeum*, No. 4667 (1919), 1015.

7 Ranjee Shahani, "T. S. Eliot: Answers and Questions," *John O'London's Weekly*, LVIII (1949), 497.

8 "Goethe as the Sage," *loc. cit.*, p. 248.

For Eliot, poetic merit or failure is explainable in terms of the presence or absence of point of view. Swinburne's verse, it is said, "appears to lack cohesion" for "there is no point of view to hold [the verse] together."[9] In Poe, "the variety and odour of his interests delight and dazzle; yet in the end the eccentricity and lack of coherence of his interests tire. There is just that lacking which gives dignity to the mature man: a consistent view of life."[10] Donne is named a "sincere" poet for he expresses a "genuine whole of tangled feeling."[11] And Pound is said to be a true "critic" of life, for he has occupied for himself a point of view from which to observe life.[12] What a poet presents is neither belief nor philosophy but a point of view, which is often by mistake called philosophy or belief[13] and which is the basis of a poet's criticism of life.

> . . . there is, it seems to me,
> At best, only a limited value
> In the knowledge derived from experience.
> The knowledge imposes a pattern and falsifies,
> For the pattern is new in every moment
> And every moment is a new and shocking
> Valuation of all we have been.[14]

Since configuration of point of view involves transmutation of feelings, organization of details, and reconciliation of conflicts, poetry may be discussed as a process of expression, unification, and resolution. In this triple line of

---

[9] "Kipling Redivivus," *loc. cit.*, p. 298.

[10] *From Poe to Valéry*, p. 19.

[11] "John Donne," *loc. cit.*, p. 332.

[12] *Ezra Pound: His Metric and Poetry*, p. 16. Also see "Introduction," *Ezra Pound: Selected Poems*, p. xxiv.

[13] "Kipling Redivivus, *loc. cit.*, p. 298.

[14] "East Coker," *Four Quartets* (New York, 1943), p. 13.

activity involved in the concentration of feelings, Eliot
finds his loci of critical argument; Correspondence, Coherence, and Comprehensiveness are, for him, the critical
triad by means of which poetic merits may be adjudged.
Moreover, consideration of breadth of view and of levels
of synthesis provides the basis for a threefold application
of each locus. Comprehensiveness, Coherence, and Correspondence each may be discussed in terms either of art,
or of the artist, or of society. "Unified sensibility," for
instance, is sometimes treated as a sign of a healthy society,
sometimes as a personal requirement of the poet, and sometimes as a condition of art. Similarly, wit is treated in the
context of art as a technical device, but as the discussion
moves upward into the realms of the requirements of the
poet and the conditions of culture, wit appears as a product
of the "maturity" of man and society; and wisdom itself
finally emerges as a divine virtue and an attribute of orthodoxy—wit, in the end, must complete itself in the "religious
comprehension of life." Not only the art work is an organized whole; society and the poet are such wholes as
well. Each work, if successful, entails a point of view, yet
all the works of a "major" poet "cohere" and exhibit an
"underlying pattern." Similarly, a poet, if he is a "significant" one, must "cohere" with tradition and "conform" to
orthodoxy—that is, he must stand as a member of the more
comprehensive whole. In expressing the "intensity" of his
own feeling, the poet, if he is a "great" one, expresses "the
intensity of feeling of his age." Since the best poetry consists in the broadest point of view and since "religious comprehension of life" is the most inclusive, the best poetry and
the true religion in the end ought to be one.

The argument is further complicated by the fact that,
according to Eliot, configuration of feeling is the process in

and by which reality is disclosed and truth is made intelligible. Eliot's critical system permits him to translate easily criticism of configuration into criticism of truth and reality. Inferior art is unreal and false because the artistic process involved is of insufficient "intensity" and the scope of unification is drastically limited. It is on the grounds of the nature of the truth and reality embodied in the configuration that Eliot ultimately distinguishes "classicism" from "romanticism." Classicism, says Eliot, is a "devotion to truth";[15] and truth and reality are the ultimate concern of criticism.[16] Speaking of Heywood, Eliot observes: "behind the motion of his personages, the shadows of the human world, there is no reality of moral synthesis"; speaking of *The Roaring Girl*, Eliot suggests: "Middleton's comedy deserves to be remembered chiefly by its real—perpetually real—and human figure of Moll the Roaring Girl."[17] It is the falsity of vision that alienates such "romantic" artists as Hardy and Lawrence from Eliot.

DYNAMICS

Eliot traces the philosophy of point of view through Bradley and Leibnitz back to Aristotle. Leibnitz's contribution, according to Eliot, lies in his treatment of the center of perception as a center of energy.

> The monad is a reincarnation of the form which is the formal cause of Aristotle. But it is also more or less. The outstanding difference is that he [Leibnitz] sets out from investigation of *physical* force, and his monads tend to become atomic centers of force.[18]

---

15 "The Letters of J. B. Yeats," *loc. cit.*, p. 90.

16 "The Function of Criticism," *loc. cit.*, p. 22.

17 "Thomas Middleton," *loc. cit.*, p. 147; "Thomas Heywood," *loc. cit.*, p. 152.

18 *Knowledge and Experience*, p. 197. Latta points out (*The Monadology and Other Philosophical Writings*, trans. Robert Latta [Oxford, 1898],

Since the whole of feeling in which finite centers are embedded is a whole, each local disturbance is bound to affect, to a large or small extent, other regions, and every finite center is subject to the pull and push of all the rest. Strictly speaking, there are an incalculable number of forces that influence the formation of a center. The situation, Eliot finds, is well described in Leibnitz's doctrine of "expression." As Eliot quotes Leibnitz:

> One thing expresses another in my use of the term when there is a constant and regulated relation between what can be said of the one and of the other. . . . Expression is common to all forms, and is a class of which ordinary perception, animal feeling, and intellectual knowledge are species. . . . Now, such expression is formed everywhere, because all substances sympathize with one another and receive some proportional change corresponding to the slightest motion in the universe.[19]

In one sense the genetic problem of poetry can never be solved, for the number of influences on the production of poetry is beyond calculation; yet for the sake of analysis Eliot finds it relevant to specify social temper, personal disposition, and artistic energy as the three basic factors that condition poetic form. Poetry, he contends, has to fulfil the demands of art, yet it is prefigured in personality and embedded in civilization. A particular society yields a particular kind of poetry. "The epic, the ballad, the chanson de geste, the forms of Provençal and of Tuscany," says Eliot, "all found their perfection by serving particular societies."[20]

---

p. 246), that Leibnitz introduced the term "point of view" in sec. 52 of his *Monadology*. "It need hardly be remarked," observes Latta, "that the term has a peculiar importance in Leibnitz's philosophy."

[19] *Knowledge and Experience*, p. 201.

[20] "The Possibility of Poetic Drama," *loc. cit.*, p. 61.

To create a form is not merely to invent a shape, a rhyme or rhythm. It is also the realization of the whole appropriate content of this rhyme or rhythm. The sonnet of Shakespeare is not merely such and such a pattern, but a precise way of thinking and feeling. The *framework* which was provided for the Elizabethan dramatist was not merely blank verse and the five-act play and the Elizabethan playhouse; it was not merely the plot—for the poet incorporated, remodelled, adapted or invented, as occasion suggested. It was also the half-formed ὕλή, the "temper of the age" (an unsatisfactory phrase), a preparedness, a habit on the part of the public, to respond to particular stimuli.[21]

Critics can best understand the poetry of a work of art through insight into the cultural environment in which it is produced and the age in which it is generated. A critic who fails to see, for instance, the "rhetoric" of the Elizabethan mind or the "sentiment" of the Victorian sensibility fails to understand the "poetry" of these times.[22]

Poetry is a "donnée" in the sense that it is moored in civilization and rooted in personality. "If you examine the works of any great innovator in chronological order," says Eliot, "you may expect to find that the author has been driven on, step by step, in his innovations, by an inner necessity, and that the novelty of form has rather been forced upon him by his material than deliberately sought."[23] And again, "the creation of a work of art, we will say the creation of a character in drama consists in the transfusion of the personality, or, in a deeper sense, the life, of the author into the character."[24] Poe's "symbolic nightmares," Eliot holds, can be accounted for by his "psychological

---

[21] *Ibid.*, p. 64.
[22] "Imperfect Critics," *loc. cit.*, pp. 30–31.
[23] *After Strange Gods*, p. 25.   [24] "Ben Jonson," *loc. cit.*, p. 118.

maladies";[25] and Milton's "magniloquence" can be traced to his musical propensity and his blindness.[26]

> The defects of a great writer's background are inextricably confused with its advantages; just as the shortcomings of his character are indissolubly associated with his shining virtues, and his material difficulties with his success. Can we regret, for instance, that François Villon did not choose to mix with more respectable society, or that Robert Burns did not have the same schooling as Dr. Johnson? The life of a man of genius, viewed in relation to his writings, comes to take a pattern of inevitability, and even his difficulties seem to have stood him in good stead.[27]

Poetry is subject to the pressure of personal constitution and social tendency, yet it must finally yield to the demand of art.

> One has prepared for art when one has ceased to be interested in one's own emotions and experiences except as material; and when one has reached this point of indifference one will pick and choose according to very different principles from the principles of those people who are still excited by their own feelings and passionately enthusiastic over their own passion.[28]

"For a poet with dramatic gifts," says Eliot, "a situation quite remote from his personal experience may release the strongest emotion"; "emotion which has never been experienced will serve its turn as well as those familiar to himself."[29] And, a poet should not be expected "to repro-

---

25 "The Approach to James Joyce," *Listener*, XXX (1943), 446.

26 "Milton I," *loc. cit.*, p. 157.

27 "The Classics and the Man of Letters," *Selected Prose*, ed. John Hayward (London, 1953), p. 224.

28 "A Brief Introduction to the Method of Paul Valéry," *loc. cit.*, p. 12.

29 "In Memoriam," *Essays Ancient and Modern* (London, 1936), p. 193; *SW*, p. 58.

duce exactly the conversational idiom of himself, his family, and his particular district."[30]

Art, artist, and circumstances each constitute a "source of vitality" for poetry. Some poetry excels because of the excellence of art (Campion's), some because of the attractiveness of the personality (Herrick's), and some because it reflects the intensity of the feeling of the time (Herbert's).[31] The best poetry, however, is the product of the coincidence of social tendency, personal predilection, and artistic energy. This happy situation Eliot characteristically describes in two movements as the conjunction of communal spirit with individual genius and as the conjunction of personality with the art.

> Hitherto, periods of great art (and in that very restricted sense, great civilization) seem always to have arisen as the unintentional and unpredictable by-product of the process of social crystallization, in which some fortunate relation (not always, by all means, the same) appears between the individual and the community.[32]

And,

> A poet's work may proceed along two lines on an imaginary graph; one of the lines being his conscious and continuous effort in technical excellence, that is, in continually developing his medium for the moment when he really has something to say. The other line is just his normal human course of development; his accumulation and digestion of experience (experience is not sought for, it is merely accepted in consequence of doing what we really want to do), and by experience I mean the results of reading and reflection, varied interests of all sorts, contacts and acquaintances, as well

---

[30] "The Music of Poetry," *loc. cit.*, p. 16.

[31] "What Is Minor Poetry?" *loc. cit.*, p. 42.

[32] "Commentary," *Criterion*, XI (1932), pp. 681, 683.

as passion and adventure. Now and then the two lines
may converge at a high peak, so that we get a master-
piece. That is to say, an accumulation of experience has
crystallized to form material of art, and years of work
in technique have prepared an adequate medium; and
something results in which medium and material, form
and content, are indistinguishable.[33]

DIRECTIONS

Local configuration of feelings involves movement; the
directions of movement afford another dimension of analysis to Eliot's criticism. Of such directions, Eliot recognizes two, the centripetal and the centrifugal. The centripetal movement yields a distinct and definite "world,"
whereas the centrifugal movement explores the inexpressible on the "borders of consciousness." Consequently Eliot
distinguishes two main types of poetry: the poetry of concentration which deals with definite "objects," and the
poetry of exploration which deals with what is beyond the
frontiers of consciousness. In his early works Eliot was
evidently in favor of the poetry of concentration, but in
his maturer years he advocated the poetry of exploration.
The decisions were made to meet the demands of what he
deemed to be the practical situations of poetic creation.
For the question he sought to answer in the first two decades of his critical career was: Where should poetry go
after Swinburne's poetry of diffusion?[34] On the other hand,
the question that haunted him in the last two decades of
his critical activity was: Where should poetry go after the
concentrated intensity of the "New Poetry"?[35] ("The gen-

---

[33] "Introduction," *Ezra Pound: Selected Poems*, p. xx.

[34] "Ezra Pound," *New English Weekly*, XXX (1946), 27.

[35] "Milton II," *loc. cit.*, p. 182; "Byron," *loc. cit.*, p. 224: "We have come
to expect poetry to be something very concentrated, something distilled. . . ."

erations of poetry in our age," observes Eliot, "seem to
cover a span of about twenty years.")[36] This difference in
practical interest results in the doctrinal differences between Eliot's two major prose collections, his *Selected Essays* and his *On Poetry and Poets*.

   To Eliot, concentration of feeling means the "qualification" and "objectification" of feeling—that is, the transmutation of the "that" into "what."[37] Concentration, in
other words, is essentially an act of abstraction and construction. To advocate the poetry of concentration is to
look for the intellectual virtues of transpicuity and precision. Thus in the earlier Eliot, the "nebulous," the
"opaque," the "vague," the "indefinite," the "inarticulate,"
and the "inexpressive" are constantly condemned and
treated as sub-poetic. Poetic emotion is, as a rule, described
as "exact," "definite," "clear," "precise," and "formulated."
For the earlier Eliot, clarity of emotion is a source of
artistic success just as opacity of emotion is a source of
poetic embarrassment. According to Eliot, the superiority
of Herbert over Vaughan, and that of Marvell over Morris
are largely a superiority of clear emotion over misty emotion. "The emotion of Herbert," says he, "is clear, definite,
mature and sustained; whereas the emotion of Vaughan
is vague, adolescent, fitful, and retrogressive."[38]

> The effect of Morris's charming poem depends upon the
> mistiness of the feeling and the vagueness of the object;
> the effect of Marvell's upon its bright, hard precision.
> And this precision is not due to the fact that Marvell
> is concerned with cruder or simpler or more carnal
> emotions. The emotion of Morris is not more refined

---

[36] "Yeats," *loc. cit.*, p. 295.

[37] *Knowledge and Experience*, esp. chap. i.

[38] "The Silurist," *loc. cit.*, p. 262.

or more spiritual; it is merely more vague; if any one doubts whether the more refined or spiritual emotion can be precise, he should study the treatment of the varieties of discarnate emotion in the *Paradiso*.[39]

"Pound's verse," says Eliot, "is always definite and concrete, because he has always a definite emotion behind it."[40] Eliot's early emphasis on the clarity of emotion has not escaped his commentator's observations. In 1930, E. K. Brown remarked that Eliot's criticism showed "a steady emphasis on *claritas, integritas, consonantia*."[41]

The doctrine of clarity is as applicable to the discussion of the style as to the discussion of emotion. In style, the early Eliot was equally in favor of the "direct," "precise," "definite," and "clear." It is his preoccupation with the "lucidity" of language that makes Eliot assert that "verse must be at least as well written as prose."[42] Moreover, it is his interest in the simple and the formal that makes the art of "caricature," of "farce," of "abstraction," of "design," his preferred art. And it is the intellectual virtues of formality and simplicity that recommend Jonson to Eliot and lead him to consider Jonson the supreme model for contemporary poets.

> Of all the dramatists of his time, Jonson is probably the one whom the present age would find the most sympathetic, if it knew him. There is a brutality, a lack of sentiment, a polished surface, a handling of large bold designs in brilliant colors, which ought to attract about

---

[39] "Andrew Marvell," *loc. cit.*, p. 258.

[40] *Ezra Pound: His Metric and Poetry*, p. 13. Cf. *SW*, p. 147, where Eliot charges that Swinburne "uses the most general word, because his emotion is never particular."

[41] E. K. Brown, "T. S. Eliot: Poet and Critic," *The Canadian Forum*, X (1930), 448.

[42] "Introduction," *Selected Poems by Marianne Moore*, p. ix.

three thousand people in London and elsewhere. At least, if we had a contemporary Shakespeare and a contemporary Jonson, it would be the Jonson who would arouse the enthusiasm of the Intelligentsia![43]

Eliot's preface to the *Transit of Venus* (1931) had already marked his shift in position.[44] But it was not until the appearance of a commentary in the *New English Weekly* for April, 1939, that he assumed the role of pleader for the poetry of exploration. For the Eliot of the forties and fifties, words cognate to "opacity," "nebulousness," "vagueness," and the like became terms of commendation rather than, as in his earlier works, of censure. In the *New English Weekly* commentary, Eliot announced his interest in "the frontiers of the spirit."[45] In "The Writer as Artist" (1940), he proposed that povetry should explore "the subtleties of thought and feeling."[46] In "Johnson as Critic" (1944), he recognized that "there is poetry which represents an attempt to extend the confines of human consciousness and to report of things unknown, to express the inexpressible."[47] And in *Poetry and Drama* (1951), he observed:

> It seems to me that beyond the nameable, classifiable emotions and motives of our conscious life when directed towards action—the part of life which prose drama is wholly adequate to express—there is a fringe of indefinite extent, of feeling which we can detect, so to speak, out of the corner of the eye and can never completely focus; of feeling of which we are only

---

[43] "Ben Jonson," *loc. cit.*, p. 121.

[44] "Preface," *Transit of Venus: Poems by Harry Crosby*, p. viii.

[45] "Commentary: That Poetry Is Made with Words," *New English Weekly*, XV (1939), 27.

[46] "The Writer as Artist," *Listener*, XXIV (1940), 774.

[47] "Johnson as Critic and Poet," *loc. cit.*, p. 193.

aware in a kind of temporary detachment from action.
. . . This peculiar range of sensibility can be expressed
by dramatic poetry, at its moments of greatest intensity.[48]

The Use of Poetry and the Use of Criticism (1933) first
recognized the "auditory imagination" as a means for the
exploration of what is "far below the conscious levels of
thought and feeling." "What I call the 'auditory imagination,' " wrote Eliot,

> is the feeling for syllable and rhythm, penetrating far
> below the conscious levels of thought and feeling, in-
> vigorating every word; sinking to the most primitive
> and forgotten, returning to the origin and bringing
> something back, seeking the beginning and the end. It
> works through meanings, certainly, not without mean-
> ings in the ordinary sense, and fuses the old and oblit-
> erated and the trite, the current, and the new and sur-
> prising, the most ancient and the most civilized men-
> tality.[49]

The "allusiveness" of poetry and the "ambiguity" of
language steadily became preoccupations of Eliot's later
critical writings. In "Andrew Marvell" (1921), Eliot insisted that the "aura" of suggestiveness cannot exist except
with "a bright, clear center."[50] But in *The Music of Poetry*
(1942) he proposed that "allusiveness" is in the nature of
words, for language must function through the most intricate of contextual qualifications and must rely upon the
subtle "music" of words, constituted by sounds and the
"secondary meanings" and "floating feelings," for its ef-
fectiveness. The poet uses language as a whole; and the

---

[48] "Poetry and Drama," *loc. cit.*, p. 93.

[49] *The Use of Poetry and the Use of Criticism*, p. 118.

[50] "Andrew Marvell," *loc. cit.*, p. 259.

meaning of words is embedded not merely in the conscious life of a people, but deeply in their unconscious. "If, as we are aware," says Eliot, "only a part of the meaning [in poetry] can be conveyed by paraphrase, that is because the poet is occupied with frontiers of consciousness beyond which words fail, though meanings still exist."[51]

The transition from an emphasis upon the lucidity of style, the clarity of visual imagination, and the formality of the poetic "world" to an emphasis upon the frontiers of consciousness, the auditory imagination, and the music and ambiguity of language is clearly reflected in Eliot's changing choice of poetic models. For instance, the earlier Eliot was preoccupied with the "wit" of Donne, a poet whose intellect dominates over the sensibility; but in 1962 Eliot's favorite topic was the "magic" of Herbert, a poet whose sensibility dominates over the intellect.[52] In the later Eliot, some poet (Dante) is given new interpretation, and some is given the same interpretation but put to a different use (Milton).

> For the real point of attack is the idolatry of a great artist by unintelligent critics, and his imitation by uninspired practitioners. A great writer can have, at a particular time, a pernicious or merely deadening influence, and this influence can be most effectively attacked by pointing out those faults which ought not to be copied, and those virtues any emulation of which is anachronistic.[53]

In "Andrew Marvell" (1921), in "John Dryden" (1921), in "The Metaphysical Poets" (1921), in "A Study of Marlowe" (1927), and even in "The Blank Verse of

---

[51] "The Music of Poetry," *loc. cit.,* p. 22.

[52] *George Herbert,* pp. 17, 18.

[53] "Introduction," *Literary Essays by Ezra Pound* (London, 1954), p. xi.

Milton" (1936), Milton's "over-cultivation" of the musical element in poetry (his "magniloquence") is condemned as a pernicious influence. Eliot never revised his formulation of the characteristics of Milton's poetry but he did change his opinion regarding the usefulness of Milton as a poetic model.[54] In his Henrietta Hertz Lecture on Milton (1947) he stated:

> Milton does, as I have said, represent poetry at the extreme limit from prose; and it was one of our tenets that verse should have the virtues of prose, that diction should become assimilated to cultivated contemporary speech, before aspiring to the elevation of poetry. Another tenet was that the subject-matter and the imagery of poetry should be extended to topics and objects related to life of a modern man or woman; that we were to seek the non-poetic, to seek even material refractory to transmutation into poetry, and words and phrases which had not been used in poetry before. And the study of Milton could be of no help here; it *was* only a hindrance.
>
> We cannot, in literature, any more than in the rest of life, live in a perpetual state of revolution. If every generation of poets made it their task to bring poetic diction up to date with the spoken language, poetry would fail in one of its most important obligations. For poetry should help, not only to refine the language of the time, but to prevent it from changing too rapidly: a development of language at too great a speed would be a development in the sense of a progressive deterioration, and that is our danger today. If the poetry of the rest of this century takes the line of development which seems to me, reviewing the progress of poetry through the last three centuries, the right course, it will discover new and more elaborate patterns of a diction now

---

[54] See E. P. Bollier, "T. S. Eliot and John Milton: A Problem in Criticism," *Tulane Studies in English*, VIII (1958), 165–92.

established. In this search it might have much to learn
from Milton's extended verse structure.[55]

No less significant is Eliot's shifting analysis of Dante's
poetry. In *Dante* (1921), Eliot treated the poet as a poet of
"visual imagination," emphasizing the clarity and precision
of his imagery, which, in Eliot's opinion, successfully co-
operates with the allegorical framework in presenting a
vision of the human soul unmatched in profundity and
comprehensiveness. *The Divine Comedy* appeared some
thirty years later in "A Talk on Dante" (1950) as a useful
model for the poetry of exploration, for it constitutes a
constant "reminder" of the duty of poetry to explore the
ever-evasive "frontiers of the spirit."

> It is therefore a constant reminder to the poet, of the
> obligation to explore, to find words for the inarticulate,
> to capture those feelings which people can hardly even
> feel, because they have no words for them; and at the
> same time, a reminder that the explorer beyond the
> frontiers of ordinary consciousness will be able to re-
> turn and report to his fellow-citizens, if he has all the
> time a firm grasp upon the realities with which they are
> already acquainted.[56]

While the centrifugal movement in experience returns
poetry to the "felt background" which is generally known
to be the realm of sensibility, the centripetal movement
brings forth a poetic "world" out of feeling by what is
usually called the intellect. Reduced to its simplicity, the
opposition between Eliot's poetry of concentration and his
poetry of exploration is basically a variation of the oppo-

---

[55] "Milton II," *loc. cit.*, pp. 182–83.

[56] "A Talk on Dante," *Kenyon Review*, XIV (1952), 188. This essay
was first published as "Talk on Dante," *Italian News*, No. 2 (July, 1950),
13–18.

sition between intellect and sensibility. Characteristics that Eliot has attributed to the poetry of concentration are intellectual virtues just as characteristics that he has found in the poetry of exploration are drawn from features of sensibility. The clarity of intellect and the subtlety of sensibility both being aspects of experience, each is supposed to be complementary to the other in the operation of experience toward an ever more inclusive Unity. Eliot advocates the poetry of clarity and the poetry of opacity at two different periods of his life; the doctrinal change, however, is neither a theoretical mutation nor an act of caprice. It is rather an orderly transition in points of emphasis in a unified account of experience. Thus, advocating the poetry of concentration in his earlier days, Eliot was yet able to observe that the "inexhaustible and terrible nebula of emotion which surrounds all our exact practical passions and mingles with them" was a source of poetic vitality.[57] And preoccupied with the poetry of exploration, he still insisted that only those who have "all the time a firm grasp upon the realities with which they are already acquainted" can return from the frontiers of consciousness and report their findings there.[58] Indeed, the whole of Eliot's criticism may be taken as a structure of categories of unification, couched in the language of configuration and dynamics and manipulated by logical disjunction and logical equation for the justification of practical poetic action.

The dialectic of Unity, for Eliot, is not only applicable to the analysis of poetry; theories of culture and education, politics and religion, all can be justified or refuted on the grounds of Unity. Culture, Eliot contends, is an organic

---

[57] "Andrew Marvell," *loc. cit.*, p. 259.
[58] "A Talk on Dante," *loc. cit.*, p. 188.

growth of value. In the course of cultural development, there are numerous motor forces working to establish centers of activity which give particular expressions to value and meaning; but meanwhile all the local centers are destined to come to terms and eventually to be assimilated into a large and inclusive pattern.[59] What has been said about the formation of the "collective personality" of a people (which is its culture), may as well be said about the cultivation of the individuals (which is their education). According to the value it is to pursue and approximate, education may be divided into three types: the professional, the social, and the individual. Professional education aims at the development of technical skills, social education aims at the development of citizens, and individual education aims at the development of human potentialities. Each level of education has its own specific purpose to accomplish, yet each is implicit in the other. "The ideal is a life in which one's livelihood, one's function as a citizen, and one's self-development all fit into and enhance each other."[60] Since the problems of education ultimately are problems of the realization and coordination of values, education is a direct concern of ethics and theology.[61] And an "educated" person is one who has "a capacity for orthodoxy."[62]

In terms of the coordination and realization of values, Eliot not only discussed culture and education but also

---

[59] *Notes towards the Definition of Culture.* Cf. "Civilization: the Nature of Cultural Relations," *Friendship, Progress and Civilization* (London, 1943), p. 17. E. R. Marks, "T. S. Eliot and the Ghost of S. T. C.," *Sewanee Review*, Vol. LXXII (1964), also noted Eliot's "organic" concept of culture.

[60] "The Aims of Education, 3," *Measure*, II (1951), 294.

[61] "The Aims of Education, 4," *Measure*, II (1951), 362–75.

[62] "A Review of Son of Woman: The Story of D. H. Lawrence," *Criterion*, X (1931), 771. Cf. "The Problem of Education," *Harvard Advocate*, CXXI (1934), 11.

politics and religion. Anglicanism is the more feasible religious position, for it approximates the virtues of both Protestantism and Ultramontanism by admitting tradition and dogma while allowing local variations.[63] In politics, Eliot upholds Bishop Bramhall against Hobbes. Bramhall, Eliot contends, recognizes degrees of reality and a hierarchy of values; consequently, although he is a fierce monarchist, he is still able to hold the king accountable as a moral being as well as a political ruler, to insist upon the balance of Church and State, and to provide room for both freedom of the will and the Grace of God. Hobbes is also a fierce monarchist, but Hobbes reduces reality to sense perceptions and confuses psychology with ethics. His monarchy is unrestrained by moral obligations, his Church is only a department of the State, and his individuals are mere atomic automatons stirring about according to the necessity of natural laws.[64] As Hobbes is a spurious Royalist, so Bramhall is a genuine one. In *For Lancelot Andrewes*, Eliot announced in one breath that in religion he was an Anglo-Catholic, in politics a Royalist, and in literature a classicist.[65] Eliot's treatment of the perfect point of view as the highest of poetry well qualifies him as a classicist as he defines it. (Classicism is a devotion to truth, reality, and value.)[66] Emending the last lacuna of his doctoral dissertation forty-

---

[63] "Thoughts after Lambeth," *SE*, pp. 321–22.

[64] "John Bramhall," *SE*, pp. 301 ff. Also see "A Commentary," *Criterion*, X (1931), 481–90; "A Commentary," *Criterion*, XI (1931), 69, 71; "A Commentary," *Criterion*, XII (1933), 642–47; "A Commentary," *Criterion*, XIII (1934), 629–30.

[65] *For Lancelot Andrewes*, p. ix.

[66] "The Letters of J. B. Yeats," *loc. cit.*, p. 90: "The classical sense is merely the devotion to truth, not decoration or personal eccentricities; the sense of values—and at the same time wholly free from Puritanism." Eliot listed truth and reality as the goals for classicism in "The Function of Criticism," *loc. cit.*, p. 22.

six years after its completion, Eliot recently wrote: "It is suitable that a dissertation on the work of Francis Herbert Bradley should end with the words 'the Absolute.' "[67] Similarly, perhaps it is suitable for a dissertation on the criticism of T. S. Eliot to conclude with the words "a Classicist."

[67] *Knowledge and Experience*, p. 11. Also see p. 176.

Bibliography

For those critical works not listed here, readers are advised to consult:

GALLUP, DONALD. *T. S. Eliot: A Bibliography*. New York: Harcourt, Brace & Co., 1953. Gallup listed Eliot's works up to December, 1951.

Critical Works by Eliot

BOOKS AND PAMPHLETS

Ezra Pound, His Metric and Poetry. New York: Knopf, 1917.

The Sacred Wood: Essays on Poetry and Criticism. London: Methuen & Co., Ltd., 1920. (2d ed., 1928.)

For Lancelot Andrewes: Essays on Style and Order. London: Faber & Gwyer, 1928.

John Dryden: The Poet, the Dramatist, the Critic. New York: Terence & Elsa Holliday, 1932.

Selected Essays: 1917–1932. New York: Harcourt, Brace & Co., 1932. (New edition, 1950.)

The Use of Poetry and the Use of Criticism: Studies in the Relation of Criticism to Poetry in England. London: Faber & Faber, 1933.

After Strange Gods: A Primer of Modern Heresy. London: Faber & Faber, 1934.

Elizabethan Essays. London: Faber & Faber, 1934.

Essays Ancient and Modern. London: Faber & Faber, 1936.

The Idea of a Christian Society. London: Faber & Faber, 1939.

The Music of Poetry. Glasgow: Jackson, Son & Co., 1942.

Four Quartets. New York: Harcourt, Brace & Co., 1943.

Die Einheit der Europäischen Kultur. Berlin: Carl Habel Verlagsbuchhandlung, 1946.

From Poe to Valéry. New York: Harcourt, Brace & Co., 1948.

Notes towards the Definition of Culture. London: Faber & Faber, 1948.

Essays by T. S. Eliot. Edited by Kazumi Yano. Tokyo: Henkyusha, 1951.

American Literature and American Language: An Address Delivered at Washington University on June 9, 1953. With an Appendix of the Eliot Family in St. Louis, Prepared by the Department of English. Washington University Studies, n.s.: Language and Literature No. 23. St. Louis: Washington University, Committee on Publications, 1953.

Selected Prose. Edited by John Hayward. London: Penguin Books in association with Faber & Faber, 1953.

Religious Drama: Mediaeval and Modern. New York: House of Books, Ltd., 1954. (Identical with Gallup c425.)

The Literature of Politics: A Lecture Delivered at a C.P.C. Literary Luncheon. London: Conservative Political Center, 1955.

Essays on Elizabethan Drama. New York: Harcourt, Brace & Co., 1956.

On Poetry and Poets. New York: Farrar, Straus & Cudahy, 1957.

George Herbert. London: Published by Longmans, Green & Co. for The British Council and the National Book League, 1962.

Knowledge and Experience in the Philosophy of F. H. Bradley. London: Faber & Faber, 1964.

To Criticize the Critic and Other Writings. New York: Farrar, Straus & Giroux, 1965.

CONTRIBUTIONS TO BOOKS

"A Brief Introduction to the Method of Paul Valéry," *Le Serpent par Paul Valéry.* Translated by Mark Wardle. London: Cobden-Sanderson, 1924. Pp. 7–15.

"Introduction," *Savonarola*, by Charlotte Eliot. London: Cobden-Sanderson, 1926. Pp. vii–xii.

"Introduction," *Ezra Pound: Selected Poems*. Edited by T. S. Eliot. London: Faber & Gwyer, 1928. Pp. vii–xxv.

"Introduction," *The Wheel of Fire*, by G. Wilson Knight. London: Oxford University Press, 1930. Pp. xi–xix.

"Donne in Our Time," *A Garland for John Donne: 1631–1931*. Edited by Theodore Spencer. Cambridge, Mass.: Harvard University Press, 1931. Pp. 1–19.

"Preface," *Transit of Venus: Poems by Harry Crosby*. Paris: Black Sun Press, 1931. Pp. i–ix.

"Preface," *Bubu of Montparnasse*, by Charles-Louis Philippe. Translated by Laurence Vail. Paris: Crosby Continental Editions, 1932. Pp. vii–xiv.

"A Critical Note," *The Collected Poems of Harold Monro*. Edited by Alida Monro. London: Cobden-Sanderson, 1933. Pp. xiii–xvi.

"Johnson's London and the Vanity of Human Wishes," *English Critical Essays: Twentieth Century*. Edited by Phyllis M. Jones. London: Oxford University Press, 1933. Pp. 301–10. First appeared as "Introductory Essay" to *London: A Poem and the Vanity of Human Wishes* by Samuel Johnson. London: Etchells & Macdonald, 1930.

"Shakespearean Criticism: From Dryden to Coleridge," *A Companion to Shakespeare Studies*. Edited by Harley Granville-Barker and G. B. Harrison. Cambridge University Press, 1934. Pp. 287–99.

"Introduction," *Selected Poems by Marianne Moore*. New York: Macmillan Co., 1935. Pp. vii–xvi.

"A Note on the Verse of Milton," *Essays and Studies by Members of the English Association*, Vol. XXI. Edited by Herbert Read. Oxford: Clarendon Press, 1936. Pp. 32–40.

"Poetry and Propaganda," *Literary Opinion in America*. Edited by M. D. Zabel. New York: Harper & Brothers, 1937. Pp. 25–38. First appeared in *Bookman*, LXX, No. 6 (February, 1930), 595–602.

"Revelation," *Revelation by Gustaf Aulén and Others.* Edited by JOHN BAILLIE and HUGH MARTIN. London: Faber & Faber, 1937. Pp. 1–39.

"A Note on Two Odes of Cowley," *Seventeenth Century Studies Presented to Sir Herbert Grierson.* Oxford: Clarendon Press, 1938. Pp. 235–42.

"Preface," *Anabasis: A Poem,* by ST. J. PERSE. New York: Harcourt, Brace & Co., 1938. Pp. 7–11. First English edition by Faber & Faber in 1930.

"A Note on War Poetry," *London Calling.* Edited by STORM JAMESON. New York: Harper & Brothers, 1942. Pp. 237–38.

"Civilization: The Nature of Cultural Relations," *Friendship, Progress, Civilization: Speeches to the Anglo-Swedish Society by Lord Sempill, Harold Nicolson, and T. S. Eliot.* London: Anglo-Swedish Society, 1943. Pp. 15–20.

"Introduction," *Shakespeare and the Popular Dramatic Tradition,* by S. L. BETHELL. Westminster: P. S. King & Staples Ltd., 1943. Pp. 7–9.

"Leçon de Valéry," *Paul Valéry.* Marseille: Cahiers du Sud, 1946. Pp. 74–81.

"Preface," *The Dark Side of the Moon.* New York: Charles Scribner's Sons, 1947. Pp. vii–x.

"Introduction," *All Hallows' Eve,* by CHARLES WILLIAMS. New York: Pellegrini & Cudahy, 1948. Pp. ix–xviii.

"Ulysses, Order, and Myth," *James Joyce: Two Decades of Criticism.* Edited by SEON GIVENS. New York: Vanguard Press, Inc., 1948. Pp. 198–202.

"Preface," *English Poetry and Its Contribution to the Knowledge of a Creative Principle,* by LEONE VIVANTE. London: Faber & Faber, 1950. Pp. vii–xi.

"Foreword," *Contemporary French Poetry,* by JOSEPH CHIARI. New York: Philosophical Library, 1952. Pp. vii–xi.

"Foreword," *Shakespeare,* by HENRI FLUCHÈRE. London: Longmans, Green & Co., 1953. Pp. vi–vii.

"Introduction," *Literary Essays by Ezra Pound.* Edited by T. S. ELIOT. London: Faber & Faber, 1954. Pp. ix–xv.

"Foreword," *Symbolism from Poe to Mallarmé, the Growth of a Myth,* by JOSEPH CHIARI. London: Rockliff, 1956. Pp. v–viii.

"Introduction," *The Art of Poetry.* (*The Collected Works of Paul Valéry,* edited by J. MATTHEWS, Vol. VII.) New York: Pantheon Books, 1958. Available in paperback edition (New York: Random House, 1961).

CONTRIBUTIONS TO PERIODICALS

"Theism and Humanism," *International Journal of Ethics,* XXVI, No. 2 (January, 1916), 284–89.
"The Development of Leibnitz's Monadism," *Monist,* XXVI, No. 4 (October, 1916), 534–56.
"Leibnitz's Monads and Bradley's Finite Centers," *Monist,* XXVI, No. 4 (October, 1916), 566–76.
"Reflections on *Vers Libre,*" *New Statesman,* VIII, No. 204 (March, 1917), 518–19.
"The Letters of J. B. Yeats," *Egoist,* IV, No. 6 (July, 1917), 89–90.
"Reflections on Contemporary Poetry I," *Egoist,* IV, No. 8 (September, 1917), 118–19.
"Reflections on Contemporary Poetry II," *Egoist,* IV, No. 9 (October, 1917), 133–34.
"Reflections on Contemporary Poetry III," *Egoist,* IV, No. 10 (November, 1917), 151.
"Disjecta Membra," *Egoist,* V, No. 4 (April, 1918), 55.
"Observations," *Egoist,* V, No. 5 (May, 1918), 69–70.
"Contemporanea," *Egoist,* V, No. 6 (June, 1918), 84–85.
"Studies in Contemporary Criticism [II]," *Egoist,* V, No. 10 (November, 1918), 131–33.
"Kipling Redivivus," *Athenaeum,* No. 4645 (May, 1919), pp. 297–98.
"Beyle and Balzac," *Athenaeum,* No. 4648 (May, 1919), pp. 392–93.
"Criticism in England," *Athenaeum,* No. 4650 (June, 1919), pp. 456–57.
"The Education of Taste," *Athenaeum,* No. 4652 (June, 1919), pp. 520–21.
"A Foreign Mind," *Athenaeum,* No. 4653 (July, 1919), pp. 552–53.
"Reflections on Contemporary Poetry IV," *Egoist,* VI, No. 3 (July, 1919), 39–40.

"Was There a Scottish Literature?" *Athenaeum*, No. 4657 (August, 1919), pp. 680–81.

"Humanist, Artist, and Scientist," *Athenaeum*, No. 4667 (October, 1919), pp. 1014–15.

"War-Paint and Feathers," *Athenaeum*, No. 4668 (October, 1919), p. 1036.

"A Brief Treatise on the Criticism of Poetry," *Chapbook*, II, No. 9 (March, 1920), 1–10.

"Modern Tendencies in Poetry," *Shama'a*, I, No. 1 (April, 1920), 9–18.

"Artists and Men of Genius," *Athenaeum*, No. 4704 (June 25, 1920), p. 842.

"Prose and Verse," *Chapbook*, XXII (April, 1921), 3–10.

"London Letter," *Dial*, LXXI, No. 2 (August, 1921), 213–17.

"London Letter," *Dial*, LXXII, No. 5 (April, 1922), 510–13.

"Notes on Current Letters: The Romantic Englishman, The Comic Spirit, and The Function of Criticism—The Lesson of Baudelaire," *Tyro*, I (1922), 4.

"Dramatis Personae," *Criterion*, I, No. 3 (April, 1923), 303–6.

"John Donne," *Nation & Athenaeum*, XXXIII, No. 10 (June, 1923), 331–32.

"The Function of a Literary Review," *Criterion*, I, No. 4 (July, 1923), 421.

"Andrew Marvell," *Nation & Athenaeum*, XXXIII, No. 26 (September, 1923), 809.

"Ulysses, Order, and Myth," *Dial*, LXXV, No. 5 (November, 1923), 480–83.

"Marianne Moore," *Dial*, LXXV, No. 6 (December, 1923), 594–97.

"A Letter to the Editor: F. M. Ford," *Transatlantic Review*, I, No. 1 (January, 1924), 95–96.

"A Commentary," *Criterion*, II, No. 7 (April, 1924), 231–35.

"The Ballet," *Criterion*, III, No. 11 (April, 1925), 441–43.

"Shakespeare and Montaigne," *Times Literary Supplement*, No. 1249 (December 24, 1925), p. 895.

"The Idea of a Literary Review," *Criterion*, IV, No. 1 (January, 1926), 1–6.

"Creative Criticism," *Times Literary Supplement*, No. 1280 (August 12, 1926), p. 535.

"Chaucer's 'Troilus,'" *Times Literary Supplement*, No. 1281 (August 19, 1926), p. 547.

"Mr. Read and Mr. Fernandez," *Criterion*, IV, No. 4 (October, 1926), 751–57.

"Whitman and Tennyson," *Nation & Athenaeum*, XL, No. 11 (December, 1926), 426.

"A Note on Poetry and Belief," *Enemy*, I (January, 1927), 15–17.

"The Problems of the Shakespeare Sonnets," *Nation & Athenaeum*, XL, No. 19 (February, 1927), 664, 666.

"Literature, Science, and Dogma," *Dial*, LXXXII, No. 3 (March, 1927), 239–43.

"A Study of Marlowe," *Times Literary Supplement*, No. 1309 (March, 1927), p. 140.

"Poet and Saint . . . ," *Dial*, LXXXII, No. 5 (May, 1927), 424–31.

"A Commentary," *Criterion*, V, No. 3 (June, 1927), 283–86.

"A Commentary," *Criterion*, VI, No. 2 (August, 1927), 97–100.

"The Mysticism of Blake," *Nation & Athenaeum*, XLI, No. 24 (September, 1927), 779.

"The Silurist," *Dial*, LXXXIII, No. 3 (September, 1927), 259–63.

"Isolated Superiority," *Dial*, LXXXIV, No. 1 (January, 1928), 4–7.

"Mr. Lucas's Webster," *Criterion*, VII, No. 4 (June, 1928), 155–58.

"Civilisation: 1928 Model," *Criterion*, VIII, No. 30 (September, 1928), 161–64.

"Introduction to Goethe," *Nation & Athenaeum*, XLIV, No. 15 (January, 1929), 527.

"Experiment in Criticism," *Bookman*, LXX, No. 3 (November, 1929), 225–33.

"Poetry and Propaganda," *Bookman*, LXX, No. 6 (February, 1930), 595–602. Reprinted in *Literary Opinions in America.*

Edited by M. D. ZABEL. New York: Harper & Brothers,
1937. Pp. 25–38.

"Thinking in Verse: A Survey of Early Seventeenth Century
Poetry," *Listener*, III, No. 61 (March, 1930), 441–43.

"Rhyme and Reason: The Poetry of John Donne," *Listener*,
III, No. 62 (March, 1930), 502–3.

"Mystic and Politician as Poet: Vaughan, Traherne, Marvell,
Milton," *Listener*, III, No. 64 (April, 1930), 590–91.

"A Commentary," *Criterion*, X, No. 40 (April, 1931), 481–90.

"A Review of Son of Woman: The Story of D. H. Lawrence," *Criterion*, X, No. 41 (July, 1931), 768–74.

"A Commentary," *Criterion*, XI, No. 42 (October, 1931),
65–72.

"The Modern Dilemma: Christianity and Communism," *Listener*, VII, No. 166 (March, 1932), 382–85.

"A Commentary," *Criterion*, XI, No. 45 (July, 1932), 676–83.

"A Commentary," *Criterion*, XII, No. 46 (October, 1932),
73–79.

"A Commentary," *Criterion*, XII, No. 47 (January, 1933),
244–49.

"A Commentary," *Criterion*, XII, No. 49 (July, 1933), 642–47.

"A Commentary," *Criterion*, XIII, No. 53 (July, 1934), 624–
30.

"The Problem of Education," *Harvard Advocate*, CXXI, No.
1 (Freshman number, 1934), 11–12.

"A Commentary," *Criterion*, XIV, No. 54 (October, 1934),
86–90.

"A Commentary," *Criterion*, XIV, No. 57 (July, 1935),
610–13.

"Views and Reviews III," *New English Weekly*, VII, No.
18 (September, 1935), 351–52.

"Literature and the Modern World," *American Prefaces*, I,
No. 2 (November, 1935), 19–22.

"Mr. Murry's Shakespeare," *Criterion*, XV, No. 61 (July,
1936), 708–10.

"A Commentary," *Criterion*, XVII, No. 66 (October, 1937),
81–86.

"A Commentary: That Poetry Is Made with Words," *New English Weekly*, XV, No. 2 (April, 1939), 27–28.

"That Poetry Is Made with Words" [a letter to the editor], *New English Weekly*, XV, No. 4 (May, 1939), 66.

"Preface to the English Tradition," *Christendom*, X, No. 38 (June, 1940), 101–8.

" 'The Duchess of Malfy,' " *Listener*, XXVI, No. 675 (December, 1941), 825–26.

" 'A Dream within a Dream': T. S. Eliot on Edgar Allan Poe," *Listener*, XXIX, No. 737 (February, 1943), 243–44.

"The Approach to James Joyce," *Listener*, XXX, No. 770 (October, 1943), 446–47.

"Ezra Pound," *Poetry*, LXVIII, No. 6 (September, 1946), 326–38.

"The Aims of Education. 1. Can 'Education' Be Defined?" *Measure*, II, No. 1 (December, 1950), 3–16.

"The Aims of Education. 2. The Interrelation of Aims," *Measure*, II, No. 2 (Spring, 1951), 191–203.

"The Aims of Education. 3. The Conflict between Aims," *Measure*, II, No. 3 (Summer, 1951), 285–97.

"The Aims of Education. 4. The Issue of Religion," *Measure*, II, No. 4 (Autumn, 1951), 362–75.

"A Talk on Dante," *Kenyon Review*, XIV, No. 1 (Winter, 1952), 178–88. First appeared as "Talk on Dante," *Italian News*, No. 2 (July, 1950), 13–18.

"On Teaching the Appreciation of Poetry," *Teachers College Record*, LXII, No. 3 (December, 1960), 215–21.

Interviews

Hodin, J. P. "T. S. Eliot on the Condition of Poetry Today: An Interview with T. S. Eliot," *Horizon*, XII, No. 68 (August, 1945), 83–89.

Breit, Harvey. "An Interview with T. S. Eliot," *New York Times Book Review*, November 11, 1948, p. 3.

Peefer, Franz. "Gesprach mit T. S. Eliot," *Rheinischer Merkur*, IV, No. 46 (1949), 7.

PELLEGRINI, ALESSANDRO. "A London Conversation with T. S. Eliot," *Sewanee Review*, LVII, No. 2 (June, 1949), 287–92.

SHAHANI, RANJEE. "T. S. Eliot: Answers and Questions," *John O'London's Weekly*, LVIII, No. 1 (August, 1949), 497–98.

HAMILTON, IAIN. "[Eliot's] Reflections on 'The Cocktail Party,' " *World Review*, n.s., No. 9 (November, 1949), pp. 19–22.

HAILEY, FOSTER. "An Interview with T. S. Eliot," *New York Times*, April 16, 1950.

HEWES, HENRY. "T. S. Eliot: Confidential Playwright," *Saturday Review*, XXXVI (August, 1953), 26–28.

LEHMANN, J. "T. S. Eliot Talks about Himself and the Drive To Create," *New York Times Book Review*, November 29, 1953, pp. 5, 44.

HEWES, HENRY. "Eliot on Eliot: Interview," *Saturday Review*, XLI (September 13, 1958), 32.

HALL, DONALD. "The Art of Poetry: T. S. Eliot," *Paris Review*, No. 21 (Winter, 1959), pp. 47–70.

Commentaries on Eliot's Criticism

BOOKS AND PARTS OF BOOKS

BEER, ERNST. *Thomas Stearns Eliot und der Antiliberalismus des XX Jahrhunderts*. Wien: W. Braumüller, 1953.

BERGSTEN, STAFFAN. *Time and Eternity: A Study in the Structure and Symbolism of T. S. Eliot's Four Quartets*. Stockholm: Boumers, 1960.

BLACKMUR, R. P. "The Danger of Authorship," *The Double Agent*. New York: Arrow Editions, 1935. Pp. 172–83.

———. "It Is Later than He Thinks," *The Expense of Greatness*. New York: Arrow Editions, 1940. Pp. 239–44.

BOYD, ERNEST. *Studies from Ten Literatures*. New York: Scribner's Sons, 1925. Pp. 315–17.

BRADBROOK, M. C. "Eliot's Critical Method," *T. S. Eliot: A Study of His Writings by Several Hands. Focus III*. Edited by B. RAJAN. London: Dennis Dobson, 1947. Pp. 119–28.

———. *T. S. Eliot*. Bibliographical Series of Supplement to British Book News No. 8. London: Longmans, Green &

Co., for the British Council and the National Book League, 1950. Pp. 44–54. (Revised ed., 1955.)

BRAYBROOKE, NEVILLE (ed.). *T. S. Eliot: A Symposium for His Seventieth Birthday.* New York: Farrar, Straus & Cudahy, 1958.

BROMBERT, VICTOR H. *The Criticism of T. S. Eliot: Problem of an "Impersonal Theory of Poetry."* New Haven: Yale University Press, 1949.

BROOK, VAN WYCK. "What Is Primary Literature?" *Opinions of Oliver Allston.* New York: E. P. Dutton & Co., 1941. Pp. 211–27.

BUCKLEY, VINCENT. *Poetry and Morality: Studies on the Criticism of Matthew Arnold, T. S. Eliot, and F. R. Leavis.* London: Chatto & Windus, 1959.

BURKE, KENNETH. "The Allies of Humanism Abroad," *The Critique of Humanism.* Edited by C. HARTLEY GRATTAN. New York: Brewer & Warren, 1930. Pp. 169–92.

COWLEY, MALCOLM. "Readings from the Lives of the Saints," *Exile's Return: A Literary Odyssey of the 1920's.* New edition. New York: Viking, 1951. Pp. 110–15.

DAICHES, DAVID. *Poetry and the Modern World.* Chicago: University of Chicago Press, 1940. Pp. 90–127.

FERGUSSON, FRANCIS. "T. S. Eliot and His Impersonal Theory of Art," *The American Caravan: A Yearbook of American Literature.* Edited by VAN WYCK BROOKS et al. New York: Macaulay, 1927. Pp. 446–53.

FERNANDEZ, RAMON. "The Classicism of T. S. Eliot," *Message.* Translated by MONTGOMERY BELGION. New York: Harcourt, Brace & Co., 1927. Pp. 295–304.

FOERSTER, NORMAN. "The Esthetic Judgment and the Ethical Judgment," *The Intent of the Critic.* Edited by D. A. STAUFFER. Princeton: Princeton University Press, 1941. Pp. 63–88.

FRANK, WALDO. "The Universe of T. S. Eliot," *In the American Jungle.* New York: Farrar & Rinehart, 1937.

FREED, LEWIS. *T. S. Eliot: Aesthetics and History.* La Salle, Ill.: Open Court, 1962.

FRYE, NORTHROP. *T. S. Eliot.* Edinburgh and London: Oliver & Boyd, 1963.

GEORGE, A. G. *T. S. Eliot: His Mind and Art.* Bombay: Asia Publishing Co., 1962.

GLICKSBERG, CHARLES I. "Thomas Stearns Eliot," *American Literary Criticism: 1900–1950.* Edited by C. I. GLICKSBERG. New York: Hendricks House, Inc., 1951. Pp. 129–33.

GREENE, EDWARD J. H. *T. S. Eliot et la France.* Paris: Doivin et Cie, 1951. Pp. 143–210.

GRUDIN, LOUIS. *Mr. Eliot among the Nightingales.* London: Joiner & Steele, 1932.

HEATH-STUBBS, JOHN. "We Have Heard the Key Turn," *T. S. Eliot: A Symposium.* Edited by RICHARD MARCH and M. J. TAMBIMUTU. Chicago: Henry Regnery, 1949.

HIGGINS, BERTRAM. "The Critical Method of T. S. Eliot," *Scrutinies II.* Edited by EDGELL RICKWOOD. London: Wishart, 1931. Pp. 54–71.

HYMAN, STANLEY EDGAR. "T. S. Eliot and Tradition," *The Armed Vision: A Study in the Methods of Modern Literary Criticism.* New York: Knopf, 1948. Pp. 33–106.

KENNER, HUGH. *The Invisible Poet: T. S. Eliot.* New York: McDowell & Obolensky, 1959. Pp. 94–123.

KRIEGER, MURRAY. *The New Apologists for Poetry.* Minneapolis: University of Minnesota Press, 1956. Pp. 46–56.

LEWIS, WYNDHAM. "T. S. Eliot, the Pseudo-Believer," *Men without Art.* London: Cassell & Co., 1934. Pp. 65–100.

LUCY, SEAN. *T. S. Eliot and the Idea of Tradition.* London: Cohen & West, 1960.

LYND, ROBERT. "Mr. T. S. Eliot as Critic," *Books and Authors.* London: Cobden-Sanderson, 1922. Pp. 248–55.

MATTHIESSEN, F. O. *The Achievement of T. S. Eliot: An Essay on the Nature of Poetry.* London: Oxford University Press, 1935. Revised ed., 1947.

MORDELL, ALBERT. *T. S. Eliot's Deficiencies as a Social Critic. T. S. Eliot—Special Pleader as Book Reviewer and Literary Critic: A Study of the Literary Leader of Intellectual, Political, Religious, and Philosophical Reaction, with Impish Glances at His Earlier Voltairean Skepticism and Free-*

Bibliography 151

Thought. Girard, Kansas: Haldeman-Julius Publications, 1951.

NOTT, KATHLEEN. *The Emperor's Clothes.* London: Heinemann, 1953.

NUHN, FERNER. "Orpheus in Hell: T. S. Eliot," *The Wind Blew from the East.* New York: Harper and Bros., 1942. Pp. 205–15.

ORAS, ANTS. *The Critical Ideas of T. S. Eliot.* Acta et Commentationes, Universitatis Tartuensis, Ülihool, B. Humaniora, xxviii, 3. Tartu: [Printed by K. Mattiesen, Ltd.], 1932.

PARKES, H. B. "T. S. Eliot," *The Pragmatic Test: Essays in the History of Ideas.* San Francisco: Colt Press, 1941. Pp. 178–86.

POUND, EZRA. "Prefatio Aut Cimicium Tumulus," "Mr. Eliot's Solid Merit," *Polite Essays.* Norfolk, Conn.: New Directions, 1937. Pp. 35–52, 98–105.

RALEIGH, JOHN H. "Revolt and Revaluation in Criticism, 1900–1930," *The Development of American Criticism.* Edited by FLOYD STOVALL. Chapel Hill: University of North Carolina Press, 1955. Pp. 59–198.

RANSOM, JOHN CROWE. "T. S. Eliot: The Historic Critic," *New Criticism.* Norfolk, Conn.: New Directions, 1941. Pp. 135–208.

RASCOE, BURTON. "Pupils of Polonius," *The Critique of Humanism.* Edited by C. HARTLEY GRATTAN. New York: Brewer & Warren, 1930. Pp. 109–30.

READ, HERBERT. *The True Voice of Feeling: Studies in English Romantic Poetry.* London: Faber & Faber, 1953. Pp. 139–50.

ROBBINS, R. H. *The T. S. Eliot Myth.* New York: H. Schuman, 1951.

SAVAGE, D. S. "The Orthodoxy of T. S. Eliot," *The Personal Principle.* London: Routledge, 1944. Pp. 91–112.

SHAPIRO, KARL. *In Defense of Ignorance.* New York: Random House, 1952.

SLOCHOWER, HARRY. *No Voice Is Wholly Lost: Writers and Thinkers in War and Peace.* New York: Creative Age Press, 1945. Pp. 181–83.

SMIDT, KRISTIAN. *Poetry and Belief in the Work of T. S. Eliot.*

Skrifter Utgitt av Det Norske Videnskaps-Akademi I Oslo II, Hist.-Filo. Klasse, 1940, No. 1. Oslo: I Okommisjo Hos Jacob Dybwad, 1949. (Revised ed.; London: Routledge & Kegan Paul, 1961.)

SMITH, BERNARD. *Forces in American Criticism.* New York: Harcourt, Brace & Co., 1939. Pp. 158–59, 382–87.

SMITH, CAROL H. *T. S. Eliot's Dramatic Theory and Practice: From Sweeney Agonistes to the Elder Statesman.* Princeton: Princeton University Press, 1963.

SMITH, LOGAN PEARSALL. *Milton and His Modern Critics.* Boston: Little, Brown & Co., 1941.

SPENDER, STEPHEN. "T. S. Eliot in His Criticism," *The Destructive Element.* London: Jonathan Cape, 1935. Pp. 153–75.

STONIER, C. W. "Eliot and the Plain Reader," *Gog, Magog and Other Critical Essays.* London: J. M. Dent & Sons, 1933. First published in *The Fortnightly Review,* CXXXVIII (1932), 620–29.

THOMPSON, ERIC. *T. S. Eliot: A Metaphysical Perspective.* Carbondale: Southern Illinois University Press, 1963.

UNGER, LEONARD (ed.) *T. S. Eliot: A Selected Critique.* New York: Rinehart, 1948.

VAN DOREN, MARK. "Mr. Eliot Glances Up," *The Private Reader.* New York: Holt, 1942. Pp. 212–16.

WILLIAMSON, GEORGE. *The Talent of T. S. Eliot.* (University of Washington Chapbooks No. 32, edited by GLENN HUGHES.) Seattle: University of Washington Bookstore, 1929.

———. "The Use of His Criticism," *A Reader's Guide to T. S. Eliot: A Poem by Poem Analysis.* New York: Noonday Press, 1955. Pp. 27–49.

WILSON, EDMUND. "T. S. Eliot," *Axel's Castle.* New York: Charles Scribner's Sons, 1931. Pp. 93–131.

WINTERS, YVOR. "T. S. Eliot, or the Illusion of Reaction," *The Anatomy of Nonsense.* Norfolk, Conn.: New Directions, 1943. Pp. 120–67.

WRIGHT, GEORGE T. *The Poet in the Poem: The Personae of Eliot, Pound, and Yeats.* Berkeley: University of California Press, 1960. Pp. 69–87.

DOCTORAL DISSERTATIONS

AUSTIN, ALLEN. "T. S. Eliot as a Literary Critic." Ph.D. dissertation, New York University, 1954.

BOLLIER, ERNEST P. "T. S. Eliot and the Idea of Literary Tradition." Ph.D. dissertation, Columbia University, 1959.

BUTZ, HAZEL E. "The Relation of T. S. Eliot to the Christian Tradition." Ph.D. dissertation, Indiana University, 1955.

COSTELLO, SISTER MARY CLEOPHAS. *Between Fixity and Flux: A Study in the Concept of Poetry and the Criticism of T. S. Eliot.* Washington, D.C.: Catholic University of America Press, 1947.

GRAHAM, JAMES C. "The Critical Theories of T. S. Eliot and I. A. Richards." Ph.D. dissertation, University of Wisconsin, 1942.

HOSKOT, S. S. *T. S. Eliot: His Mind and Personality.* Bombay: University of Bombay, 1961. Pp. 139–40.

PANICKER, GEEVARGHESE T. "A Whole of Feeling: A Study of the Place of Emotion and Feeling in the Poetic Theory of T. S. Eliot." Ph.D. dissertation, Catholic University of America, 1959. (Abstract available in pamphlet form.)

ROONEY, FR. WILLIAM JOSEPH. *The Problem of "Poetry and Belief" in Contemporary Criticism.* Washington, D.C.: Catholic University of America Press, 1949.

SCOTT, PETER D. "The Social and Political Ideas of T. S. Eliot." Ph.D. dissertation, McGill University, 1955.

SHAW, SAM. "T. S. Eliot's Theory of Tradition." Ph.D. dissertation, New York University, 1964.

THEALL, DONALD F. "Communication Theories in Modern Poetry: Yeats, Pound, Eliot, Joyce." Ph.D. dissertation, University of Toronto, 1955.

THOMPSON, MARION C. "The Dramatic Criticism of T. S. Eliot." Ph.D. dissertation, Cornell University, 1953.

WATERS, LEONARD. "Coleridge and Eliot: A Comparative Study of Their Theories of Poetic Composition." Ph.D. dissertation, University of Michigan, 1948.

WILLIAMSON, MERVYN W. "A Survey of T. S. Eliot's Criticism: 1917–1956." Ph.D. dissertation, University of Texas, 1958.

PERIODICAL ARTICLES

AIKEN, CONRAD. "The Poetic Dilemma," *Dial*, LXXXVII, No. 5 (May, 1927), 420–23.

ARAKAWA, T. "T. S. Eliot's Interpretation of Arnold and Pater," *Studies in English Literature*, XIII (1933), 161–81.

ASTRE, GEORGES-ALBERT. "T. S. Eliot et la nostalgie de la 'culture,' " *Critique*, V (Summer, 1949), 774–811.

AUSTIN, ALLEN. "T. S. Eliot's Objective Correlative," *University of Kansas City Review*, XXVI, No. 2 (Winter, 1959), 133–40.

BARRY, IRIS. "The Ezra Pound Period," *Bookman*, LXXIV, No. 2 (October, 1931), 159–71.

BATES, E. S. "T. S. Eliot, Leisure Class Laureate," *Modern Monthly*, VII (February, 1933), 17–24.

BATESON, F. W. "Dissociation of Sensibility," *Essays in Criticism*, I, No. 3 (July, 1951), 302–12.

BELL, CLIVE. "T. S. Eliot," *Nation & Athenaeum*, XXXIII, No. 25 (September, 1923), 772–73.

BIRRELL, FRANCIS. "The Poetic Drama Once More," *Nation & Athenaeum*, XLIII, No. 14 (July, 1928), 470.

BLACKMUR, R. P. "Homage to T. S. Eliot," *Harvard Advocate*, CXXV, No. 3 (December, 1938), 20.

———. "Mr. Eliot and Notions of Culture: A Discussion," *Partisan Review*, XI, No. 3 (Summer, 1944), 302–4.

BLISETT, WILLIAM. "Pater and Eliot," *University of Toronto Quarterly*, XXII, No. 3 (April, 1953), 261–68.

BOLLIER, E. P. "T. S. Eliot and John Milton: A Problem in Criticism," *Tulane Studies in English*, VIII (1958), 165–92.

BOVEY, J. A. "The Literary Criticism of T. S. Eliot," *American Prefaces*, I, No. 4 (January, 1936), 67–71.

BROMBERT, VICTOR. "T. S. Eliot and the Romantic Heresy," *Yale French Studies*, XIII (Spring, 1954), 3–6.

BROWN, E. K. "T. S. Eliot: Poet and Critic," *The Canadian Forum*, X, No. 120 (September, 1930), 448.

BROWN, WALLACE C. "T. S. Eliot and the Demon of the Ego," *The New Humanist*, VIII, No. 3 (Summer, 1935), 81–85.

------. "Mr. Eliot without the Nightingales," *University of Kansas City Review*, XIV, No. 1 (Autumn, 1947), 31–38.

CAMPBELL, HARRY M. "An Examination of Modern Critics: T. S. Eliot," *Rocky Mountain Review*, VIII, No. 3 (Spring, 1944), 128–37.

CATLIN, GEORGE. "T. S. Eliot and the Moral Issue," *Saturday Review*, XXXII, No. 2 (July, 1949), 7–8, 36–38.

CHASE, RICHARD. "The Sense of the Present," *Kenyon Review*, VII, No. 2 (Spring, 1945), 218–31.

------. "T. S. Eliot in Concord," *American Scholar*, XVI, No. 4 (Autumn, 1947), 438–43.

CHILD, RUTH C. "The Early Critical Works of T. S. Eliot: An Assessment," *College English*, XII, No. 5 (February, 1951), 269–75.

CHURCH, R. W. "Eliot on Bradley's Metaphysics," *Harvard Advocate*, CXXV, No. 3 (December, 1938), 24–26.

COLLINS, W. E. "T. S. Eliot the Critic," *Sewanee Review*, XXIX, No. 4 (October, 1931), 419–24.

COWLEY, MALCOLM. "The Religion of Art: Readings from the Lives of the Saints," *New Republic*, LXXVII, No. 996 (January, 1934), 216–18.

CURTIS, ERNST ROBERT. "T. S. Eliot als Kritiker," *Die Literatur*, XXXII, No. 1 (October, 1929), 11–15.

CZAMANSKE, PALMER, *et al.* "The Beginning of T. S. Eliot's Theory of Culture," *Cresset*, XV, No. 9 (July, 1952), 9–21.

DAICHES, DAVID. "T. S. Eliot," *Yale Review*, XXXVIII, No. 3 (March, 1949), 460–70.

DANIELLS, J. R. "T. S. Eliot and His Relation to T. E. Hulme," *University of Toronto Quarterly*, II, No. 3 (April, 1933), 380–96.

D'ARCY, M. C. "The Thomistic Synthesis and Intelligence," *Criterion*, VI, No. 3 (September, 1927), 210–28.

DAVIS, ROBERT G. "The New Criticism and the Democratic Tradition," *American Scholar*, XIX, No. 1 (Winter, 1949), 9–19.

DUNKEL, W. D. "T. S. Eliot's Quest for Certitude," *Theology Today*, VII, No. 2 (July, 1950), 228–36.

EASTMAN, MAX. "The Swan Song of Human Letters," *Scribner's*, LXXXVIII, No. 6 (December, 1930), 598–607.

ELLIOTT, G. R. "T. S. Eliot and Irving Babbitt," *The American Review*, VII, No. 4 (September, 1936), 442–54.

FALCK, COLIN. "Hurry Up Please! It's Time," *The Review*, No. 4 (November, 1962), pp. 59–64.

FLUCHÈRE, HENRI. "L'Attitude Critique de T. S. Eliot," *Cahiers du Sud*, XXXV, No. 292 (2ᵐᵉ Semestre, 1948), 499–511.

GEORGE, R. E. GORDON. "The Return of the Native," *Bookman*, LXXV, No. 5 (September, 1932), 423–31.

GLICKSBERG, CHARLES I. "T. S. Eliot as Critic," *Arizona Quarterly*, IV, No. 3 (Autumn, 1948), 225–36.

GREENBERG, CLEMENT. "Mr. Eliot and Notions of Culture: A Discussion," *Partisan Review*, XI, No. 3 (Summer, 1944), 305–7.

———. "T. S. Eliot: The Criticism, the Poetry," *The Nation*, CLXXI, No. 24 (December, 1950), 531–33.

HARA, ICHIRO. "Poetry and Belief: Richards vs. Eliot," *Studies in English Literature*, XV (1935), 221–44.

HAUSERMANN, HANS W. "T. S. Eliot's Conception of Poetry," *Études de Lettres*, XVI, No. 4 (October, 1942), 165–78.

HAWKINS, DESMOND. "Hamlet and T. S. Eliot," *New English Weekly*, XV, No. 25 (October, 1939), 312–13.

HENNECKE, HANS. "T. S. Eliot: Der Dichter als Kritiker," *Europäische Revue*, XII, No. 9 (September, 1936), 721–35.

HILLYER, ROBERT. "Poetry's New Priesthood," *Saturday Review*, XXXII, No. 25 (June, 1949), 7–9, 38.

HUTCHINS, ROBERT M. "T. S. Eliot on Education," *Measure*, I, No. 1 (Winter, 1950), 1–8.

JULIAN, CONSTANCE. "T. S. Eliot and the Anglo-Catholics," *The Fireside*, XII, No. 8 (August, 1946), 11–14.

KNICKERBOCKER, WILLIAM S. "Bellwether, an Exercise in Dissimulatio," *Sewanee Review*, XLI, No. 1 (January, 1933), 64–79.

KRONENBERGER, LOUIS. "T. S. Eliot as Critic," *The Nation*, CXL, No. 3641 (April, 1935), 452–53.

LEAVIS, F. R. "T. S. Eliot's Status as Critic," *Commentary*, XXVI (November, 1958), 399–410.

———. "Mr. Eliot and Mr. Milton," *Sewanee Review,* LVII, No. 1 (January, 1949), 1–30.

LEBOWITZ, MARTIN. "Thought and Sensibility," *Kenyon Review,* V, No. 2 (Spring, 1943), 219–27.

LORING, M. L. S. "T. S. Eliot on Matthew Arnold," *Sewanee Review,* XLIII, No. 4 (October, 1935), 479–88.

LUCAS, F. L. "Criticism," *Life and Letters,* III, No. 18 (November, 1929), 433–65.

MCELDERLY, B. R. "Santayana and Eliot's 'Objective Correlative,' " *Boston University Studies in English,* III (Autumn, 1957), 178–81.

MANGAN, SHERRY. "A Note: On the Somewhat Premature Apotheosis of Thomas Stearns Eliot," *Pagany,* I, No. 2 (Spring, 1930), 23–36.

MARKS, E. R. "T. S. Eliot and the Ghost of S. T. C.," *Sewanee Review,* LXXII (Spring, 1964), 262–80.

MARX, LEO. "Mr. Eliot, Mr. Trilling and Huckleberry Finn," *American Scholar,* XXII, No. 4 (Autumn, 1953), 423–40.

"Milton Lost and Regained," *Times Literary Supplement,* No. 2356 (March 29, 1947), p. 140.

MOLONEY, M. F. "Mr. Eliot and Critical Tradition," *Thought,* XXI, No. 82 (September, 1946), 455–74.

———. "The Critical Faith of Mr. T. S. Eliot," *ibid.,* XXII, No. 85 (June, 1947), 297–341.

MOORMAN, CHARLES. "Order and Mr. Eliot," *South Atlantic Quarterly,* LII, No. 1 (January, 1953), 73–87.

MORROW, FELIX. "The Serpent's Enemy: Mr. More as Social Thinker," *Symposium,* I, No. 2 (April, 1930), 168–93.

MUIR, EDWIN. "T. S. Eliot," *The Nation,* CXXI, No. 3135 (August, 1925), 162–64. (Reprinted in Muir's *Transition* [New York: Viking Press, 1926]. Pp. 131–46.)

MURRY, J. M. "Towards a Synthesis," *Criterion,* V, No. 3 (September, 1927), 297–313.

NICOLL, ALLARDYCE. "Eliot and the Revival of Classicism," *College English,* XXIII, No. 4 (April, 1934), 269–78.

PARKINSON, THOMAS. "Intimate and Impersonal: An Aspect of Modern Poetics," *Journal of Aesthetics and Art Criticism,* XVI, No. 3 (March, 1958), 373–83.

PHILLIPS, W. "Mr. Eliot and Notions of Culture: A Discussion," *Partisan Review,* XI, No. 3 (Summer, 1944), 307–9.

PRAZ, MARIO. "T. S. Eliot and Dante," *Southern Review,* II, No. 3 (Winter, 1937), 525–48. (Reprinted in *The Scottish Review,* I, No. 2 [Summer, 1948], 30–51.)

QUENNELL, PETER. "Mr. T. S. Eliot," *Life and Letters,* II, No. 10 (March, 1929), 179–90.

REES, GARNET. "A French Influence of T. S. Eliot: Rémy de Gourmont," *Revue de Littérature Comparée,* XVI, No. 4 (October, 1936), 764–67.

"Reflections," *Time,* LV, No. 10 (March, 1950), 22–26.

RICHARDS, I. A. "Mr. Eliot and Notions of Culture: A Discussion," *Partisan Review,* XI, No. 3 (Summer, 1944), 310–12.

ROUSSEAUX, ANDRÉ. "Poésie et Poétique de T. S. Eliot," *Figaro Littéraire,* V (May, 1950), 2.

SCHAPPES, MORRIS. "The Irrational Malady," *Symposium,* I, No. 4 (October, 1950), 518–30.

SCHWARTZ, DELMORE. "The Criterion: 1922–1939," *Kenyon Review,* I, No. 4 (Autumn, 1939), 437–49.

———. "The Literary Dictatorship of T. S. Eliot," *Partisan Review,* XVI, No. 2 (February, 1949), 119–37.

SHAPIRO, K. "T. S. Eliot: The Death of Literary Judgment," *Saturday Review,* XLIII (February, 1960), 12–17.

SHAPIRO, LEO. "The Mediaevalism of Eliot," *Poetry: A Magazine of Verse,* LVI, No. 4 (July, 1940), 202–13.

SMITH, GROVER, JR. "Getting Used to T. S. Eliot," *College English,* XLIX, No. 1 (January, 1960), 1–10, 15.

STALLMAN, R. W. *The Critic's Notebook.* Minneapolis: University of Minnesota Press, 1950. Pp. 116, 118.

STEADMAN, JOHN M. "Eliot and Husserl: The Origin of the 'Objective Correlative,'" *Notes and Queries,* CCIII (June, 1958), 261–62.

STONIER, G. W. "Eliot and the Plain Reader," *Fortnightly Review,* CXXXVIII (November, 1932), 620–29.

STRONG, ROBERT. "The Critical Attitude of T. S. Eliot," *London Quarterly and Holborn Review,* CLVIII (October, 1933), 513–19.

STUART, D. A. "Modernistic Critics and Translators," *Princeton Library Bulletins*, II (Summer, 1950), 177–78.

"T. S. Eliot Goes Home," *Living Age*, CCCXLII, No. 4388 (May, 1932), 234–36.

TAUPIN, RENÉ. "The Example of Rémy de Gourmont," *Criterion*, X, No. 41 (July, 1931), 614–25.

———. "The Classicism of T. S. Eliot," translated by LOUIS ZUKOFSKY, *Symposium*, III, No. 1 (January, 1932), 64–84.

THOMAS, R. HINTON. "Culture and T. S. Eliot," *Modern Quarterly*, n.s. VI, No. 2 (Spring, 1951), 147–62.

THOMPSON, ERIC. "Dissociation of Sensibility," *Essays in Criticism*, II (April, 1952), 207–13.

TILLYARD, E. M. W. "The Personal Heresy in Criticism: A Rejoinder," *Essays and Studies by Members of the English Association*, XX (1934), 7–20.

TINDALL, WILLIAM YORK. "T. S. Eliot in America: The Recantation of T. S. Eliot," *American Scholar*, XVI, No. 4 (Autumn, 1947), 432–37.

TURNELL, G. M. "Tradition and Mr. T. S. Eliot," *Colosseum*, I, No. 2 (June, 1934), 44–54.

VIVAS, ELISEO. "The Objective Correlative of T. S. Eliot," *American Bookman*, I, No. 1 (Winter, 1944), 7–18. (Reprinted in *Critiques and Essays in Criticism: 1920–1948*. Edited by ROBERT W. STALLMAN. New York: Ronald, 1949. Pp. 389–400.)

VOIGHT, F. A. "Milton, Thou Shouldst Be Living," *The Nineteenth Century*, CXXX (October, 1941), 211–21.

WECTER, DIXON. "The Harvard Exiles," *Virginia Quarterly Review*, X, No. 2 (April, 1934), 244–57.

WEISS, TED. "Eliot and the Courtyard Revolution," *Sewanee Review*, LIV, No. 2 (Spring, 1946), 289–307.

WELLEK, RENÉ. "The Criticism of T. S. Eliot," *Sewanee Review*, LXIV, No. 3 (Summer, 1956), 398–443.

WILLIAMS, RAYMOND. "T. S. Eliot on Culture," *Essays in Criticism*, VI, No. 3 (July, 1956), 302–18.

WILLIAMSON, GEORGE. "The Talent of T. S. Eliot," *Sewanee Review*, XX, No. 3 (July, 1927), 284–95.

WILLIAMSON, H. R. "T. S. Eliot and His Conception of Poetry," *Bookman*, LXXIX, No. 474 (March, 1931), 347–50.

WILSON, EDMUND. "Mr. More and the Mithraic Bull," *New Republic*, XCI, No. 1173 (May, 1937), 64–68.

SELECTED REVIEWS

AIKEN, CONRAD. "The Scientific Critic," *The Freeman*, II, No. 51 (March, 1921), 593–94. (*The Sacred Wood.*)

———. "For Lancelot Andrewes," *Dial*, XXCVI, No. 7 (July, 1929), 628.

———. "After Ash Wednesday," *Poetry: A Magazine of Verse*, XLV, No. 3 (December, 1934), 161–65. (*After Strange Gods.*)

———. "Mr. Eliot in the Wilderness," *New Republic*, LXXXVIII, No. 1142 (October, 1936), 326–27. (*Essays Ancient and Modern.*)

ANAND, MULK RAJ. "Mr. Eliot's Kipling," *Life and Letters Today*, XXXII, No. 55 (March, 1942), 165–70. (*A Choice of Kipling's Verse.*)

ARNS, KARL. "T. S. Eliot: After Strange Gods," *Englische Studien*, LXIX (January, 1935), 420.

AUDEN, W. H. "Port and Nuts with the Eliots," *The New Yorker*, XXV, No. 9 (April, 1949), 85–87. (*Notes towards the Definition of Culture.*)

BELGION, MONTGOMERY. "The Use of Poetry," *Dublin Review*, CXCIV, No. 388 (January, 1934), 151–53. (*The Use of Poetry and the Use of Criticism.*)

———. "After Strange Gods," *Dublin Review*, CXCIV, No. 389 (April, 1934), 320–24.

BENÉT, WILLIAM ROSE. "T. S. Eliot and Original Sin," *Saturday Review*, X (May, 1934), 673–78. (*After Strange Gods.*)

BLACKMUR, R. P. "T. S. Eliot in Prose," *Poetry: A Magazine of Verse*, XLII, No. 1 (April, 1933), 44–49. (*John Dryden; Selected Essays.*)

———. "The Dangers of Authorship," *Hound and Horn*, VII, No. 4 (July, 1934), 719–26. (*After Strange Gods.*)

——. "In the Hope of Straightening Things Out," *Kenyon Review*, XIII, No. 2 (Spring, 1951), 303–14. (*Selected Essays*, new ed.) Reprinted in *The Lion and Honeycomb*, New York: Harcourt, Brace & Co., 1955.

BROOKS, CLEANTH. "The Crisis in Culture," *Harvard Alumni Bulletin*, LII, No. 18 (1950), 768–72. (*Notes towards the Definition of Culture.*)

CALVERTON, V. F. "T. S. Eliot, An Inverted Marxism," *Modern Monthly*, VIII, No. 6 (July, 1934), 372–73. (*After Strange Gods.*)

CORMICAN, L. A. "Mr. Eliot and Social Biology," *Scrutiny*, XVII, No. 1 (September, 1950), 2–13. (*Notes towards the Definition of Culture.*)

DAVIS, ROBERT G. "Culture, Religion, and Mr. Eliot," *Partisan Review*, XVI, No. 7 (July, 1949), 750–53. (*Notes towards the Definition of Culture.*)

EDMAN, IRWIN. "Notes towards the Definition of Culture," *New York Times Book Review*, March 6, 1949.

EVERY, GEORGE. "Christian Polity," *Purpose*, XII, No. 1 (January, 1940), 31–37. (*The Idea of a Christian Society.*)

——. "Mr. Eliot and the Classics," *New English Weekly*, XXVI, No. 22 (March, 1945), 191. (*What Is a Classic?*)

FERGUSSON, FRANCIS. "Golden Candlesticks," *Hound and Horn*, II, No. 3 (April, 1929), 297–99. (*For Lancelot Andrewes.*)

FORSTER, E. M. "T. S. Eliot and His Difficulties," *Life and Letters*, II, No. 13 (June, 1929), 417.

FRANK, WALDO. "The Universe of T. S. Eliot," *New Republic*, LXXII, No. 934 (October, 1932), 294–95. (*Selected Essays.*)

GARY, F. "Dante," *Symposium*, I, No. 2 (April, 1920), 268–71.

GREENWOOD, E. B. "On Poetry and Poets," *Essays in Criticism*, III, No. 3 (July, 1958), 319–24.

GREGORY, HORACE. "The Man of Feeling," *New Republic*, LXXIX, No. 1015 (May, 1934), 23–24. (*The Use of Poetry and the Use of Criticism; After Strange Gods.*)

——. "Authority of T. S. Eliot," *Commonweal*, LXVII, No. 6 (November, 1957), 148–50. (*On Poetry and Poets.*)

HARDING, D. W. "Mr. Eliot at Harvard," *Scrutiny*, II, No. 3 (December, 1933), 289–92. (*The Use of Poetry and the Use of Criticism.*)

———. "Christian or Liberal," *Scrutiny*, VIII, No. 3 (December, 1939), 309–13. (*The Idea of a Christian Society.*)

HAZLITT, HENRY. "The Mind of T. S. Eliot," *The Nation*, CXXXV, No. 3509 (October, 1932), 312–13. (*Selected Essays.*)

HODGSON, R. A. "Tradition and Mr. Eliot," *New English Weekly*, XIX, No. 23 (September, 1941), 221. (*Points of View*, ed. JOHN HAYWARD.)

HOOK, SIDNEY. "The Dilemma of T. S. Eliot," *The Nation*, CLX, No. 3 (January, 1945), 69–71. (*Notes towards the Definition of Culture.*)

HOUSE, HUMPHREY. "Mr. Eliot as a Critic," *The New Oxford Outlook*, I, No. 1 (May, 1933), 95–105. (*Selected Essays.*)

KENNER, HUGH. "Notes towards the Definition of Culture," *Hudson Review*, II, No. 2 (Summer, 1949), 289–94.

KNIGHT, L. C. "Shakespeare and Shakespeareans," *Scrutiny*, III, No. 3 (December, 1934), 306–14. (*Elizabethan Essays.*)

KRUTCH, JOSEPH WOOD. "A Poem is a Poem," *The Nation*, CXXXVII, No. 3571 (December, 1933), 679–80. (*The Use of Poetry and the Use of Criticism.*)

LEAVIS, F. R. "Mr. Eliot, Mr. Wyndham Lewis, and Lawrence," *Scrutiny*, III, No. 2 (September, 1934), 184–91. (*After Strange Gods.*)

———. "Mr. Eliot and Education," *ibid.*, V, No. 1 (June, 1936), 84–89. (*Essays Ancient and Modern.*)

———. "T. S. Eliot's Stature as Critic," *Commentary*, XXVI, No. 5 (November, 1958), 399–410. (*On Poetry and Poets.*)

LEIGHTON, L. "Eliot and Dante," *Hound and Horn*, III, No. 3 (April, 1930), 442–44. (*Dante.*)

LUNN, HUGH KINGSMILL. "Goethe, Wordsworth, and Mr. Eliot," *English Review*, LVII, No. 12 (December, 1933), 667–70. (*The Use of Poetry and the Use of Criticism.*)

"Mr. Eliot's New Essays," *Times Literary Supplement*, No. 1401 (December 6, 1928), p. 953. (*For Lancelot Andrewes.*)

MOORE, MARIANNE. "The Sacred Wood," *Dial*, LXX, No. 3 (March, 1921), 336–39.
MORE, P. E. "The Cleft Eliot," *Saturday Review*, IX, No. 17 (November, 1932), 233. (*Selected Essays*.)
MURRY, JOHN MIDDLETON. "The Sacred Wood," *New Republic*, XXVI, No. 332 (April, 1921), 194–95.
———. "The Return of the 'Mayflower,'" *New Adelphi*, II, No. 3 (March, 1929), 195–98. (*For Lancelot Andrewes*.)
OLSON, ELDER. "A Defense of Poetry," *Poetry: A Magazine of Verse*, L, No. 1 (April, 1937), 54–56.
PARKES, HENRY B. "T. S. Eliot," *Hound and Horn*, VI, No. 2 (January, 1933), 350–56. (*John Dryden; Selected Essays; L. GRUDIN's Mr. Eliot among the Nightingales*.)
PARSONS, I. M. "Mr. Eliot's Authority," *Spectator*, CXLIX, No. 5441 (October, 1932), 450–52. (*Selected Essays*.)
POCOCK, D. F. "Symposium on Mr. Eliot's 'Notes,'" *Scrutiny*, XVII, No. 3 (December, 1950), 273–76.
"A Poet's Shoptalk," *Time*, LXX, No. 12 (September, 1957), 125–26. (*On Poetry and Poets*.)
POUND, EZRA. "Mr. Eliot's Mare's Nest," *New English Weekly*, IV, No. 21 (March, 1934), 307–9. (*After Strange Gods*.)
———. "What Price the Muses Now?" *ibid.*, V, No. 6 (May, 1934), 130. (*The Use of Poetry and the Use of Criticism*.)
RAGO, HENRY. "T. S. Eliot on Culture," *Commonweal*, L, No. 5 (May, 1949), 122–25. (*Notes towards the Definition of Culture*.)
RANSOM, JOHN CROWE. "T. S. Eliot on Criticism," *Saturday Review*, X, No. 36 (March, 1934), 574. (*The Use of Poetry and the Use of Criticism*.)
RATNER, JOSEPH. "T. S. Eliot and Totalitarianism," *Saturday Review*, XXI, No. 11 (January, 1940), 7. (*The Idea of Christian Society*.)
READ, HERBERT. "Mr. Eliot's New Book," *Hudson Review*, II, No. 2 (Summer, 1949), 285–89. (*Notes towards the Definition of Culture*.)
RECKITT, MAURICE. "A Sub-Christian Society," *New English Weekly*, XVI, No. 8 (December, 1939), 115–16. (*The Idea of a Christian Society*.)

RICE, PHILIP BLAIR. "The Critic as Prophet," *Poetry: A Magazine of Verse*, L, No. 1 (April, 1937), 51–54. (*Essays Ancient and Modern.*)

RICKWOOD, EDGELL. "Selected Essays by T. S. Eliot," *Scrutiny*, I, No. 4 (March, 1933), 390–93.

ROBSON, W. W. "Eliot's Later Criticism," *The Review*, I, No. 4 (November, 1962), 51–57. (*On Poetry and Poets.*)

SALMON, CHRISTOPHER. "Critics and Criticism," *The Nineteenth Century and After*, CXV, No. 685 (March, 1934), 359–69. (*The Use of Poetry and the Use of Criticism.*)

SCHAPPES, MORRIS U. "T. S. Eliot Moves Right," *Modern Monthly*, VII (August, 1933), 403–8. (*Selected Essays; John Dryden.*)

SHUSTER, GEORGE N. "Mr. Eliot Returns," *Commonweal*, XVI, No. 25 (October, 1932), 581–83. (*Selected Essays.*)

SISSON, C. H. "What Is Culture?" *New English Weekly*, XXXIV, No. 8 (December, 1948), 91–92. (*Notes towards the Definition of Culture.*)

TATE, ALLAN. "Taste and Mr. Johnson," *New Republic*, LXVIII, No. 827 (August, 1931), 23–24. ("Introductory Essay" to *London and the Vanity of Human Wishes.*)

TRILLING, LIONEL. "Elements That Are Wanted," *Partisan Review*, VII, No. 5 (September, 1940), 367–79. (*The Idea of a Christian Society.*)

———. "Mr. Eliot's Kipling," *The Nation*, CLVII, No. 16 (October, 1943), 436–42. (*A Choice of Kipling's Verse.*)

TROY, WILLIAM. "T. S. Eliot and the Grand Inquisitor," *The Nation*, CXXXVIII, No. 3590 (April, 1934), 478–79. (*After Strange Gods.*)

VAN DOREN, MARK. "England's Critical Compass," *The Nation*, CXII, No. 2913 (May, 1921), 751.

WILSON, EDMUND. "T. S. Eliot and the Church of England," *New Republic*, LVIII, No. 751 (April, 1929), 283–84. (*For Lancelot Andrewes.*)

WOLLHEIM, R. "Eliot, Bradley and Immediate Experience," *New Statesman*, LXVII (March 13, 1964), 401–2.

W[OOLF], L. "Back to Aristotle," *Athenaeum*, No. 4729 (December, 1920), 834. (*The Sacred Wood.*)

GENERAL WORKS

ABRAMS, M. H. *The Mirror and the Lamp: Romantic Theory and the Critical Tradition.* New York: Oxford University Press, 1953.

BRADLEY, F. H. *Appearance and Reality.* 2d ed. London: Swan Sonnenschein & Co., 1906.

———. *Essays on Truth and Reality.* Oxford: Clarendon Press, 1914.

———. *Ethical Studies.* 2d ed. Oxford: Clarendon Press, 1927.

CHURCH, RICHARD. *Bradley's Dialectics.* London: G. Allen, 1942.

COLLINGWOOD, R. G. *Essay on Philosophical Method.* Oxford: Clarendon Press, 1933.

CRANE, R. S. (ed.). *Critics and Criticism: Ancient and Modern.* Chicago: University of Chicago Press, 1951.

———. "Two Essays in Practical Criticism: Prefatory Note," *University of Kansas City Review,* VIII (Spring, 1942), 199–202.

"Dialectic." *The Great Ideas: A Syntopicon of Great Books of the Western World.* (*Great Books of the Western World,* edited by ROBERT M. HUTCHINS, Vol. II.) Chicago: Encyclopaedia Britannica, 1952.

GREGORY, JOSHUA. *A Short History of Atomism: From Democritus to Bohr.* London: A. & C. Black, Ltd., 1931.

KOPNIN, P. "Dialectic," *Soviet Studies in Philosophy,* I, No. 4 (November, 1963), 16–22.

LEIBNITZ, GOTTFRIED WILHELM. *The Monadology and Other Philosophical Writings.* Translated with Introduction and Notes by ROBERT LATTA. Oxford: Clarendon Press, 1898.

McKEON, RICHARD. "The Philosophical Bases of Art and Criticism," *Critics and Criticism.* Edited by R. S. CRANE. Chicago: University of Chicago Press, 1951.

———. "Philosophy and Method," *Journal of Philosophy,* XLVII, No. 22 (October, 1951), 653–82.

———."Rhetoric and Poetic in the Philosophy of Aristotle," *Aristotle's Poetics and English Literature.* Edited by ELDER OLSON. Chicago: University of Chicago Press, 1965.

SIMON, YVES. "On Order in Analogical Sets," *New Scholasticism*, XXXIV, No. 1 (January, 1960), 1–42.

SINAIKO, HERMAN. *Love, Knowledge, and Discourse in Plato: Dialogue and Dialectic in Phaedrus, Republic, Parmenides.* Chicago: University of Chicago Press, 1965.

WICK, WARNER. *Metaphysics and the New Logic.* Chicago: University of Chicago Press, 1948.

Index